Obamacare:

A HANDBOOK FOR EMPLOYERS

*Anthony Presley, Erik van Gilder,
Jacqueline Kafka, and Audrey Presley*

Illustrated by Rebecca Scott

*With contributions by Kevin Van,
Kristen Vander Plas, and Jessica Castner*

www.EmployersAndObamacare.com

TimeForge
3008 50th Street, Suite E
Lubbock, TX 79413
www.TimeForge.com

Ordering Information:
Quantity sales. Special discounts are available on quantity purchases by corporations, associations, and others. For details, contact the publisher at the address above.
Orders by U.S. trade bookstores and wholesalers. Please contact TimeForge: Tel: (866) 684-7191; Fax: (866) 684-7191 or visit www.TimeForge.com.

Printed in the United States of America

TimeForge.
Obamacare : A Handbook for Employers / TimeForge; with Anthony Presley, Jacqueline Kafka, and Audrey Presley; Illustrated by Rebecca Scott.
ISBN-13: 978-0-615889764
ISBN-10: 061588976X
1. Affordable Care Act. 2. Business. 3. Healthcare.
I. Title.

First Edition

14 13 12 11 10 / 10 9 8 7 6 5 4 3 2 1

Acknowledgements

Just like any project of sufficient size, this book project has had dozens involved, and it may not be possible to list everyone who has helped out from day one.

We started this project to help our customers – without your support it wouldn't have been possible. Thanks for your dedication!

The TimeForge Team:
Stephanie Presley and Kali van Gilder without you we couldn't do the "hard work."

Jacqueline Kafka for spearheading the entire project.

Audrey Presley for ensuring that our brand and customers were center stage.

Rebecca Scott for constant graphical revisions based on the whims of politicians.

Jessica Castner for jumping in and ordering the chaos.

Clare Jones for lending a critical eye in a busy time.

The ABC Team:
Kevin Van for your tireless dedication to educate businesses on the new rules.

Kristen Vander Plas for editing our tired ramblings even at the last minute.

John Claborn for your insight on future directions of the legislation.

Federal Government
President Obama and the 111th Congress because without you, this entire body of work would not exist.

A Letter from TimeForge

Dear Employer,

Thank you for purchasing *Obamacare: A Handbook for Employers.* We sincerely hope it will make Obamacare easier to understand and assist you in determining how this legislation affects your business.

In this book, we will discuss how this Act affects businesses as well as individuals. You will learn how to tell if you are considered a small or large employer under the Act, how to determine the full- or part-time status of your employees, and what penalties you could receive from the IRS.

Please note that the information presented in this book is not intended to be taken as tax or legal advice. You should always consult with a competent tax advisor, insurance agent, and/or attorney before making changes that affect your business. New regulations may have been enacted since the publication of this book. These regulations may make some of the information in the book outdated. Please refer to our updates, government notices, and our website for up-to-date information.

Sincerely,

Anthony Presley
Founder
www.TimeForge.com

Praise from Texas Lt. Governor David Dewhurst

The [Obamacare] legislation is a sprawl of red tape and confusing regulations that can not only harm your organization, but also put your people at a disadvantage, so it'll pay to be prepared. Resources like *Obamacare: A Handbook for Employers* that shed some light on the details of Obamacare so you can make better decisions and take the proper action are a must.

While I have every confidence that we can keep the Texas economy strong with our emphasis on low taxes, tight spending and economic freedom, your ability to navigate the details of Obamacare will help your organization stay out of trouble with the federal government.

...I hope you'll stay informed, focus on wellness and keep your people protected with your grasp of the issues.

David Dewhurst
Lieutenant Governor of Texas

TABLE OF CONTENTS

INTRODUCTION

Obamacare, formally known as the Patient Protection and Affordable Care Act (PPACA) or the Affordable Care Act (ACA), was signed into law March 23, 2010. One of its primary goals is to make healthcare insurance affordable to all Americans. As a result, Obamacare requires all individuals to either have health insurance or pay a tax. The Supreme Court determined that this mandate is constitutional on June 28, 2012 under Congress' ability to tax its citizens. Obamacare is here to stay, and for most businesses, that means you need to understand this law so that you are not surprised by thousands of dollars in penalties, most of which begin in 2015.

COMMON MYTHS

There are many details which are misunderstood regarding Obamacare. Regardless of your political leanings, everyone admits that the government has not done a very good job of getting information about mandates and regulations to employers. If they had done a good job, you would not be reading this book! Our goal with this book is to assist you in identifying misconceptions and to help you understand what will be required.

Myth #1: Break It Into Pieces!

You may believe that if you split your businesses, or say, make your daughter or friend an owner of one of your businesses, then you will not be considered a large employer. This is not true. Large employer status is calculated on a group basis. This means that multiple businesses owned by common owners are calculated together. More information about common ownership can be found in Chapter 2, under the group basis section.

Myth #2: 50 Is The Magic Number?

Another common Obamacare myth is that if you employ 50 employees, then you are considered a large employer. This misconception does not account for part-time and full-time employees. Part-time employees are converted to a full-time equivalent (FTE), and this is combined with your number of full-time employees to determine large employer status. This is what decides whether you need to offer your full-time employees affordable healthcare coverage. The IRS will be leveling penalties on a monthly basis - although the law states an annual penalty. Chapter 2 will explore the FTE and the distinction between large and small employers.

Note:

Large Employer Status determines whether you are required to offer health insurance to your full-time employees.

Myth #3: Small Businesses Get A Tax Credit.

Similarly, you may think that if you employ less than 50 employees, then you are automatically eligible for a tax credit to help pay for affordable healthcare coverage for employees. Again, this fails to consider part-time and full-time employees. Employers eligible for a small employer tax credit can only have 25 or fewer full-time equivalent employees. Chapter 8 details the requirements to receive a Small Employer Tax Credit.

Myth #4: Reducing Hours Will Save You.

You may have heard that you can avoid Obamacare by changing most of your employees to part-time employees or all of your employees to full-time employees. However, that tactic rarely works. If all of your employees are full-time and you have 50 or more employees, you will still be penalized for not offering your employees affordable healthcare coverage. Likewise, if all but a few of your employees are part-time, and your total full-time and full-time equivalent count is 50 or more, then you still must offer that handful of full-time employees affordable health insurance. Penalties are discussed further in Chapter 3.

Myth #5: Insurance Will Be Affordable.

A misconception that applies to both employers and individuals is that healthcare costs will automatically decrease. Some individuals may be eligible for premium tax credits, which will help them pay for health insurance and their costs may decrease. However, the overall costs of healthcare continue to increase. The insurance costs released in California, which was the first state to implement Obamacare guidelines, show a rise in premium rates of up to 146%. [1] It is unknown whether the trend of increasing premiums will be ongoing, but you should expect at east an initial increase.

Myth #6: It's Not My Problem.

Like many employers, you might be adhering to a "head in the sand" approach. Ignoring Obamacare won't save you

---

1   *Roy, A. (2013, May 30). Rate shock: In California, Obamacare to increase individual health insurance premiums by 64-146%. Retrieved from http://www. forbes.com/sites/theapothecary/2013/05/30/rate-shock-in-california-obamacare-to-increase-individual-i nsurance-premiums-by-64-146/*

from the effects of the legislation, nor the penalties. In fact, the more you ignore it, the more likely you are to pay excessive penalties. It's time to stop procrastinating and get a game plan together. You might think that Obamacare is not your problem, or that another person in the company is responsible. This is not the case.

The law will create new responsibilities for employees in every division of your company. Regardless of whether you are Human Resources personnel or an Operations professional, you will likely be responsible for helping your company comply with Obamacare. More information about how Obamacare will affect every department of every company is addressed in Chapter 11.

The confusion about Obamacare may lead many people to face penalties and taxes unexpectedly, but we hope this guide will ensure you're not one of those people. The intention of this entire book is to inform you about Obamacare and prepare you, so you can avoid unnecessary risks and penalties.

PARTS OF THE BOOK

Obamacare will have many far-reaching implications for individuals as well as businesses. Both of these situations will be discussed in this guide.

The first part of the book is devoted to businesses and will help identify whether you will be classified as a large employer under Obamacare. It will also describe the penalties you may accrue if you do not offer your full-time employees affordable health insurance that provides the minimum value and standard of care described under the law.

The second part of this book is devoted to individuals and

small businesses. You will learn what type of insurance individuals are required to carry and what taxes they may have to pay if they don't have insurance. You will also learn about your potential to receive a tax credit, to help pay for your employees' costs of insurance if you are a qualified small employer under Obamacare.

The third part of this book details the new regulations which insurance companies must follow and where employers can buy insurance. Each state will have an exchange, created by the state or the federal government. The exchanges are scheduled to open October 1, 2013. The individual exchanges will provide a marketplace for individuals to shop for healthcare coverage. The Small Business Health Options Program (SHOP) will provide a marketplace for small group employers (those with up to 100 employees) to purchase healthcare coverage for their employees. The SHOPs are scheduled to open in 2014 for employers with fewer than 50 employees, and in 2016 for employers with up to 100 employees. An exchange for employers with more than 100 employees is expected to be created by 2017.

The fourth part is about how to integrate all of the information you've obtained in parts 1-3. This will include applicable examples to work through as well as copies of new federal forms (if available you will need to be aware of). Consider it a practical how-to guide to addressing Obamacare in your unique situation.

How to Read this Book

Begin with Ch.1 to familiarize yourself with Obamacare's principles.

Proceed to Ch. 2 to determine if you are a large employer.

Are you a large employer according to Ch. 2?

Yes — Proceed to Part 1 to learn about penalties and reporting regulations.

No — Proceed to Part 2 to learn about individuals and small businesses.

Continue to Part 3 to learn about insurance regulations.

Turn to Part 4 to learn about what to do now that you know all of this.

Continue to Part 3 to learn about insurance regulations.

Finish with Chapters 12, 13, and 14 to read scenarios, examples, and answers to common questions.

PART 1:
BUSINESSES

1

A TIMELINE OF
OBAMACARE

Although a large part of Obamacare has already begun, there is still much more to come. Obamacare was signed into law March 23, 2010 and the Supreme Court upheld the constitutionality of the Act on June 28, 2012. Since then, many of the provisions have already been implemented.

In 2010, small employers that met certain requirements became eligible for tax credits to help pay for health insurance for their employees.[1] The tax credits will continue to be available, and will increase over time. More information about the small employer tax credit is in Chapter 8.

Beginning in 2012, employers that provided employees with health insurance were required to provide those employees with a Summary of Benefits and Coverage, detailing the specifics of their healthcare plan. More information about the Summary of Benefits and Coverage is in Chapter 6.

Exchanges are scheduled to open October 2013, providing individuals with an online marketplace to shop for insurance. Exchanges are supposed to make it easier for customers to compare insurance plans and assess all options in one

---

1   *United Healthcare Services, INC. (2013, February 23). Timeline of provisions. Retrieved from http://www.uhc.com/united_for_reform_resource_center/ health_reform_provisions.htm*

place. Individual exchanges are described in greater detail in Chapter 9. Employers will also be required to notify their employees about the existence of exchanges by October 1, 2013. Notices that employers must provide to employees are outlined in Chapter 6.

Also beginning in 2013, employers with more than 250 employees will be required to report the cost of health insurance on W-2s so that the employee is informed about his coverage costs. Additionally, small business exchanges called Small Business Health Options Programs (SHOPs) will be open to employers with up to 50 full-time equivalent employees. The SHOPs will gradually open up to employers with more employees, allowing business owners with up to 100 full-time equivalent employees to purchase insurance in 2016. SHOPs are explained further in Chapter 9.

2014 marks the beginning of the individual mandate. This mandate requires all individuals to have health insurance or receive a penalty tax. The individual mandate is discussed in Chapter 8.

Employers will begin to accept some of the responsibility of health insurance by being required to provide health insurance to all full-time employees beginning in 2015. This is called shared responsibility and large employers who choose not to provide their full-time employees with health insurance will be penalized. Large employers and shared responsibility are covered in Chapter 3.

Finally, exchanges for employers with more than 100 full-time equivalent employees are expected to be created by 2017.

To take a look at a timeline of Obamacare, refer to pages 22-23.

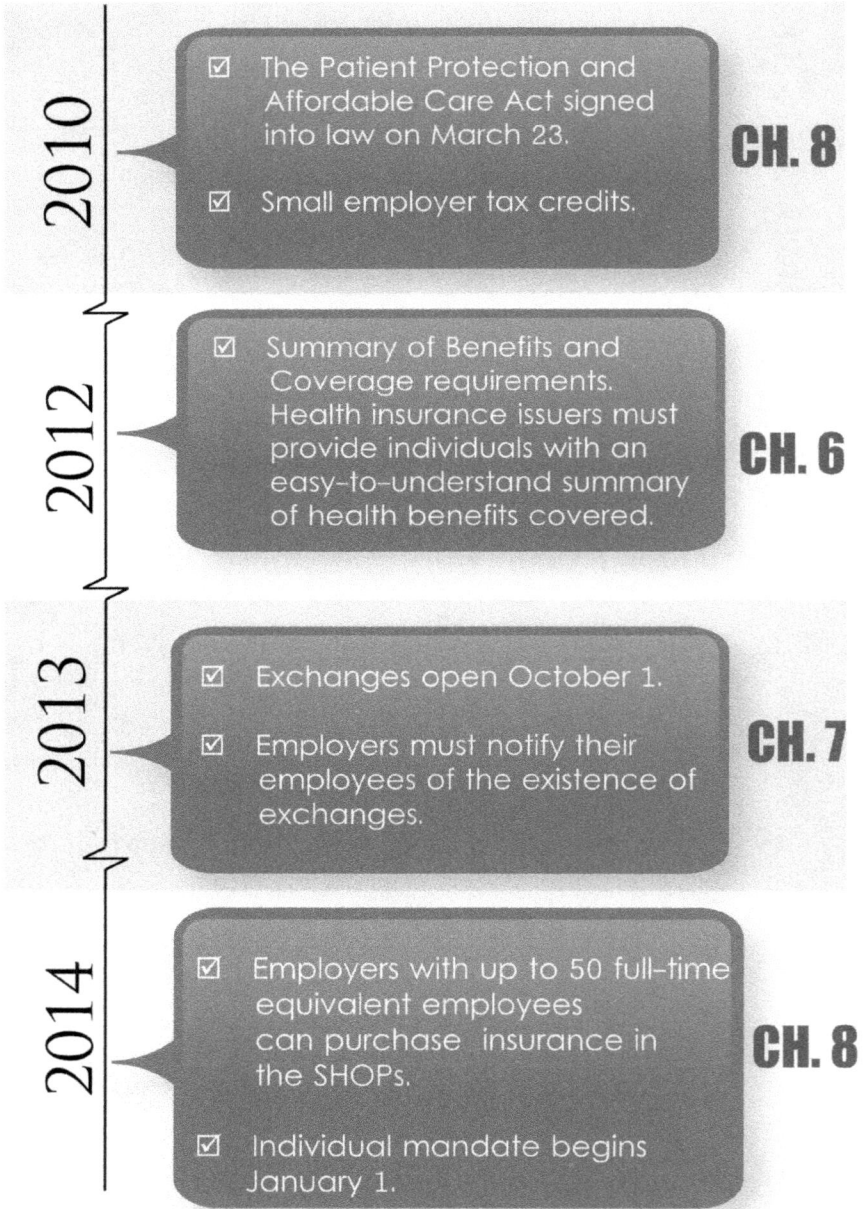

2010

☑ The Patient Protection and Affordable Care Act signed into law on March 23.

☑ Small employer tax credits.

CH. 8

2012

☑ Summary of Benefits and Coverage requirements. Health insurance issuers must provide individuals with an easy-to-understand summary of health benefits covered.

CH. 6

2013

☑ Exchanges open October 1.

☑ Employers must notify their employees of the existence of exchanges.

CH. 7

2014

☑ Employers with up to 50 full-time equivalent employees can purchase insurance in the SHOPs.

☑ Individual mandate begins January 1.

CH. 8

CH. 3

☑ Penalty is assessed for employers who do not provide minimum value and affordable coverage to full-time employees.

2015

CH. 8

☑ Employers with more than 100 full-time equivalent employees may purchase insurance in SHOPs.

2016

CH. 9

☑ States can allow businesses with more than 100 full-time equivalent employees to purchase insurance from newly created large company SHOPs.

2017

2
Large Employers and Shared Responsibility

WHAT IS A LARGE EMPLOYER?

Many of the stipulations and regulations regarding businesses and Obamacare start with determining whether you are a "large employer" or a "small employer." Obamacare treats each group differently with regard to shared responsibility of healthcare coverage. However, at the time this guide was written, some of the specifics have yet to be ironed out between the Department of Health and Human Services (HHS) and the Internal Revenue Service (IRS).

Currently, Obamacare defines a large employer as any business with an average of 50 or more full-time (FT) and full-time equivalent (FTE) employees for the prior calendar year. Therefore, every January, you need to determine your large employer status (FT + FTE) by calculating your FT + FTE average for each month of the previous year, then averaging the months together. More details on this calculation are given later in this chapter, but it's important to first understand the definitions of a FT employee and a FTE employee.

You are a Large Employer if:

Your full-time employees plus your full-time equivalent
employees equals 50 or more

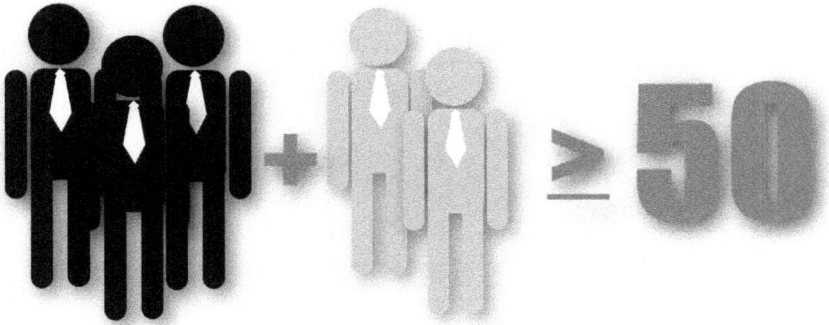

FULL-TIME EMPLOYEES

FT employees are defined as employees who work an average
of 30 hours per week or 130 hours during a calendar month,
according to the IRS regulations.[1] This standard differs
from the Family and Medical Leave Act (FMLA) and the US
Department of Labor, which both state that FT employees
must work 40 hours a week. You must be careful of this
distinction, especially when hiring PT employees. Under
Obamacare, for the purposes of calculating FT and FTE staff
members, any employee who works at least 30 hours a week
or 130 hours a month is FT. Your number of FT employees
is simply a head count of everybody who works at least 30
hours a week or 130 hours per month.

You'll find that throughout this book, we often only use the
monthly option to calculate the FT status, and disregard the
weekly. Since the IRS accepts the monthly calculation, and

---

1   *Internal Revenue Service. (2011, May 23). Request for comments on
shared responsibility for employers regarding health coverage (section 4980h).
Retrieved from http://www.irs.gov/irb/2011-21_IRB/ar07.html*

the IRS will be the agency assessing penalties, we've chosen to primarily use the monthly calculation. However, you need to be aware of upcoming clarifications about the 30 hours per week guideline. Additionally, it is currently difficult (if not impossible) to calculate FT status on a weekly basis, as there is not yet any clarification as to what a "week" is considered to be. Should the 30 hours per week be calculated based on the work week? The calendar week? If employees are hired mid-week, should you "prorate" their hours that week?

MONTHLY CALCULATION

Add up all employee hours worked during the month

	September					
Su	Mo	Tu	We	Th	Fr	Sa
28	29	30	31	1	2	3
4	5	6	7	8	9	10
11	12	13	14	15	16	17
18	19	20	21	22	23	24
25	26	27	28	29	30	1

= 130 hours

VS.

WEEKLY CALCULATION BY WORK WEEK

Store A's work week begins on Saturdays

	February					
Su	Mo	Tu	We	Th	Fr	Sa
26	27	28	29	30	31	1
2	3	4	5	6	7	8
9	10	11	12	13	14	15
16	17	18	19	20	21	22
23	24	25	26	27	28	1

or

WEEKLY CALCULATION BY CALENDAR WEEK

Some weeks are not 7 days

	September					
Su	Mo	Tu	We	Th	Fr	Sa
28	29	30	31	1	2	3
4	5	6	7	8	9	10
11	12	13	14	15	16	17
18	19	20	21	22	23	24
25	26	27	28	29	30	

The disparity between calendar and work weeks may not appear complicated in the above figure, but let's take a closer look at the hours.

In the first example below, an employee works an average of 30 hours per week during the month of February, but the hours only add up to 120 hours for the month. This is less than the 130 hour threshold used for the monthly calculation to determine if an employee is part-time or full-time. The employee in this example is FT when calculated on a weekly basis, but PT when calculated monthly. Should the employer include this in its large employer calculations as FT or PT/FTE?

EXAMPLE 1:
Work Week Calculation

Store A begins their work week on Saturdays

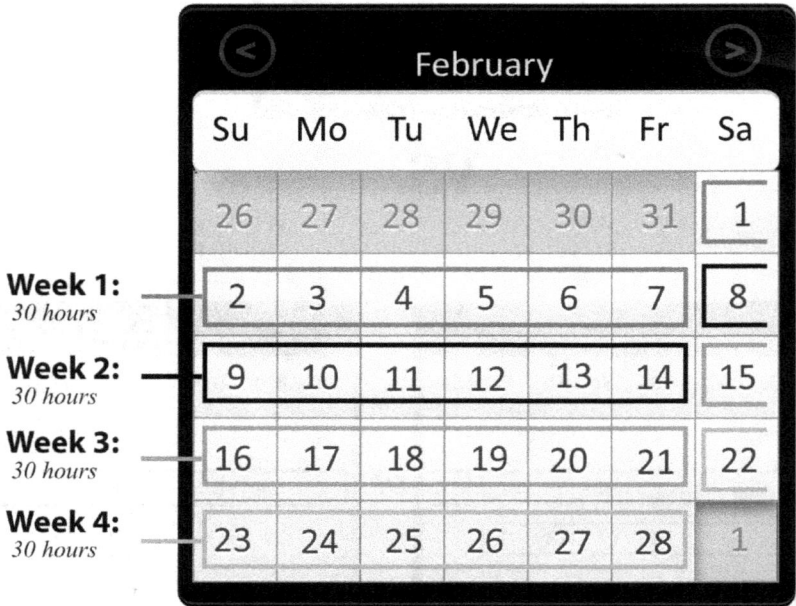

Su	Mo	Tu	We	Th	Fr	Sa
26	27	28	29	30	31	1
2	3	4	5	6	7	8
9	10	11	12	13	14	15
16	17	18	19	20	21	22
23	24	25	26	27	28	1

February

Week 1: *30 hours*
Week 2: *30 hours*
Week 3: *30 hours*
Week 4: *30 hours*

Total: *120 hrs*

In the second example, an employee works an average of less than 30 hours a week for the month of September, but still works 130 hours for the month. The employee in this example is PT when calculated on a weekly basis, but FT when calculated monthly. Should the employer include this employee in its large employer calculations as FT or PT/ FTE?

EXAMPLE 2:
Calendar Week Calculation

Su	Mo	Tu	We	Th	Fr	Sa	
28	29	30	31	1	2	3	**Week 1:** *18 hours*
4	5	6	7	8	9	10	**Week 2:** *29 hours*
11	12	13	14	15	16	17	**Week 3:** *29 hours*
18	19	20	21	22	23	24	**Week 4:** *29 hours*
25	26	27	28	29	30	1	**Week 5:** *25 hours*

September

Weekly Average: *26 hrs*
Total hours: *130 hrs*

WHAT CONSTITUTES A FULL-TIME EMPLOYEE?

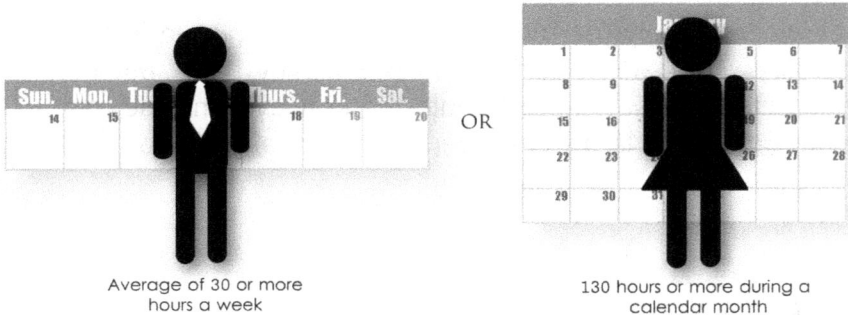

Average of 30 or more hours a week

OR

130 hours or more during a calendar month

Salaried and Exempt Employees: Do salaried or overtime exempt employees count toward your FT number? The IRS provides guidelines for calculating whether these employees are FTs or FTEs. For these employees, assign one work day the value of 8 hours, and one work week the value of 40 hours.[2] Then, add the number of hours they worked (or took paid leave), and apply the same 130 hours per month rule used to determine FT status for hourly employees.

Paid Leave: It is important to note that the IRS proposes that you include paid leave in FT employee calculations. If an employee had paid sick leave (or jury duty, paid vacation, holiday pay, etc.), then the hours for which the employee is paid while not at work must be included in the calculations.[3]

For example, an employee takes sick leave for a day and is paid for 8 hours of sick time that day. Those 8 hours of paid sick leave count toward the calculations that determine whether that employee is FT or PT.

---

2   *Internal Revenue Service. (2011, June 9). Request for comments on shared responsibility for employers regarding health coverage (section 4980h). Retrieved from http://www.irs.gov/pub/irs-drop/n-11-36.pdf*
3   *Internal Revenue Service. (2011, June 9). Request for comments on shared responsibility for employers regarding health coverage (section 4980h). Retrieved from http://www.irs.gov/pub/irs-drop/n-11-36.pdf*

New Hires: When determining whether a new employee is FT for the purposes of calculating large employer status, your judgment plays an important role. If a new employee is hired and you expect the new employee to work at least 30 hours a week or at least 130 hours a month, then the employee is likely FT. [4]

FULL-TIME EQUIVALENT

The Full-Time Equivalent (FTE) calculation converts PT employee hours worked into a relative number of FT positions occupied by those hours. The formula for determining your FTE varies as the IRS and the Affordable Care Act each define FTE differently. Specifically, the Affordable Care Act interprets the FTE based on 30-hours per week. The IRS intends to assess penalties based on 130-hours per month. However, there is an incentive to hire full-time employees, as the IRS calculation for FTE uses 120 hours, not 130 hours.

The FTE calculation is an average. The FTE is calculated on a monthly basis by determining the total number of hours worked by PTs in a month and dividing that by 120.[5] This formula converts those PT employees into a FT number, or "the FTE." Then, these averages for each month are added up and divided by 12, to determine the average FTE for the year. If the result contains a decimal, round down.

4   *Internal Revenue Service. (2012, January 1). Frequently asked questions from employers regarding automatic enrollment, employer shared responsibility, and waiting periods. Retrieved from http://www.irs.gov/pub/irs-drop/n-12-17.pdf*
5   *Internal Revenue Service. (2011, May 23). Request for comments on shared responsibility for employers regarding health coverage (section 4980h). Retrieved from http://www.irs.gov/irb/2011-21_IRB/ar07.html*

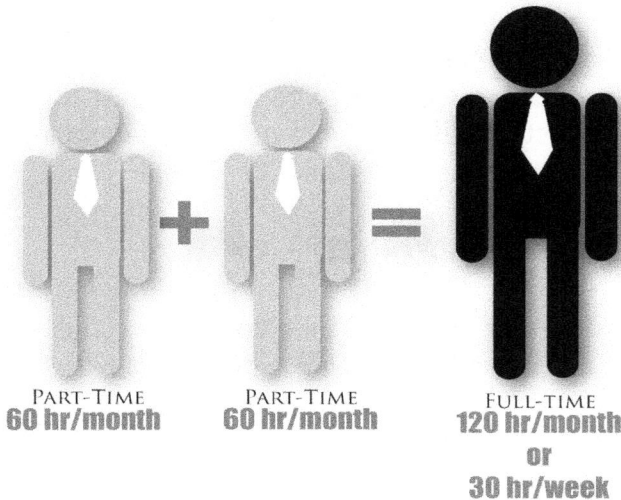

PART-TIME
60 hr/month

PART-TIME
60 hr/month

FULL-TIME
**120 hr/month
or
30 hr/week**

The FTE is determined based on PT employee hours, or all the hours worked by people who are not FT. Because of this, PT employees can significantly influence large employer status. Simply cutting everyone's hours and hiring more PT will likely not affect your FTE calculation or large employer status. The total hours your PTs are collectively working each month determines the FTE calculations.

CALCULATING LARGE EMPLOYER STATUS

Step 1. Finding the FT

Calculate the number of FTs you employed during the prior calendar year.

According to the law, "The term 'full-time employee' means, with respect to any month, an employee who is employed on average at least 30 hours of service per week", which can be found in section 1513 (section 4, paragraph A). The IRS has added that 130 hours per calendar month is also considered FT.[6] Any employee who works more than 30 hours in a week **or** more than 130 hours in a calendar month is considered full-time when determining large employer status. Any employee who didn't work an average of 30 hours per week during the month is considered PT for the determination of large employer status and will be counted in Step 2.

Step 2. Finding the FTE

To calculate FTEs for the same month, add up all of the hours worked by part-time employees during the month (not greater than 130 per employee) and divide the total by 120. The resulting calculation should be rounded down (or just remove the decimal portion), and this number is the number of FTE employees for the month. FTE is the derived calculation of the number of part-time (PT) employees it takes to work the equivalent number of hours that a FT employee works.

Step 3. Finding the monthly FT and FTE

For each month, add your FT total and your FTE total together. Set it aside for now. Don't lose it – you'll need it again. Work your way through the rest of the calendar year, writing down each month's total.

Step 4. Finding the average for the year.

Add up all twelve months' totals, then divide by 12. If the resulting number contains a decimal, round down.[7]

---

6   *Department of the Treasury. (2012, December 27). Shared responsibility for employers regarding health coverage. Retrieved from http://www.irs.gov/pub/newsroom/reg-138006-12.pdf*
7   *Department of the Treasury. (2012, December 27). Shared responsibility for employers regarding health coverage. Retrieved from http://www.irs.gov/pub/newsroom/reg-138006-12.pdf*

If this result is 50 or more, you are considered a large employer under Obamacare. If you have an average of 49 or fewer employees, you are not considered a large employer under Obamacare.

Note:

Having fewer than 50 FT+FTEs does not make you a small employer. It simply means you are not a large employer. Small employers have fewer than 25 FT+FTEs. Refer to Chapter 8.

If you have seasonal employees, please refer to the section titled "Seasonal Employee Exemption" later in this chapter for further instructions.

Future modifications to the rules regarding large employer status are expected to be issued after January 1, 2014. Unfortunately, that deadline will leave employers little time to react, since the large employer calculation period for 2015 starts during the 2014 calendar year. Even if you are not a large employer, you need to keep abreast of the future clarifications.

Under Obamacare, any business classified as a large employer is required to offer affordable insurance to FT employees or face penalties for failing to do so.[8] It is important to note here that if you qualify as a large employer, you are not required to offer insurance to any PT employees. This is why many large employers are hiring more employees, but cutting everyone's hours. Regardless of your game plan, it will become increasingly important to monitor not only the number of staff, but also staff hours, including both FT and

---

8   *Internal Revenue Service. (2011, May 23). Request for comments on shared responsibility for employers regarding health coverage (section 4980h). Retrieved from http://www.irs.gov/irb/2011-21_IRB/ar07.html*

FTE employees during the year. Improper calculations can result in heavy penalties, as discussed in the next chapter.

If you are not a large employer, you are not required to offer health insurance to your employees, but you will be directly affected by Obamacare through the individual shared responsibility, reporting requirements, and potentially the small employer tax credit. If your business is near the 50 FT + FTE mark, make sure to monitor employee hours and large employer status. Staying below the 50 FT + FTE threshold can prevent you from being classified as a large employer and being forced to offer affordable insurance to all FT employees or pay the penalties.

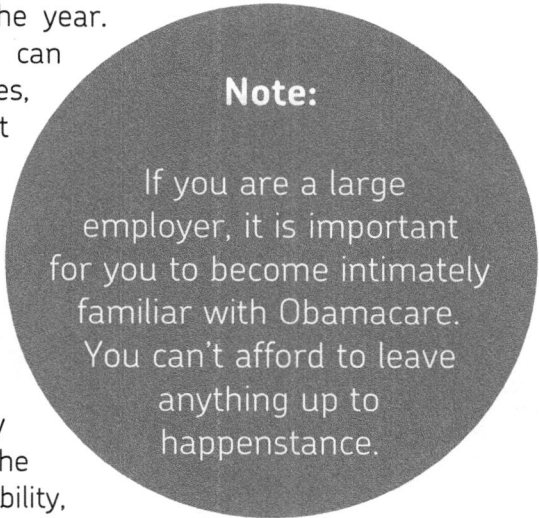

Note:

If you are a large employer, it is important for you to become intimately familiar with Obamacare. You can't afford to leave anything up to happenstance.

Whether you're a large employer or not, each year (starting in 2014), your staffing levels will determine whether or not the business will be a large employer for the upcoming year.

The number of people employed the prior year determines large employer status for the next year. So, for example, your 2014 FT and FTE will determine your large employer status for 2015. If you want to avoid being classified as a large employer for the 2015 calendar year, you will want to start calculating and monitoring FTs and FTEs before January 2014. Regardless of whether you are trying to stay below the 50 FT + FTE mark, all employers will need to calculate their FTs and FTEs from January 2014 to December 2014 to determine large employer status for 2015.

It is unclear whether the large employer calculation locks in large employer status for the next year. The IRS implies that if your business is determined to be a small employer based on the previous year, and goes over 50 FT + FTE employees sometime during the current year, then you will not be penalized for not offering affordable healthcare coverage to FT employees, because you were determined to be a small employer.[9] However, because the IRS merely implies this and does not appear to have clearly defined whether an employer is "locked" into their large or small employer status for the whole year, industry experts are divided on whether the IRS will penalize small employers who exceed the 50 FT + FTE employee mark for a short period of time. Just to be safe, if you are close to the 50 FT + FTE mark, you should monitor your number of employees to make sure you stay below the large employer threshold, at least until the IRS provides more guidance on how they will assess penalties.

Example:

A business with 53 FT + FTE employees in the 2014 year will be considered a large employer for the 2015 calendar year. And, a business with 49 employees in the 2015 year will be considered a small employer for the 2016 calendar year.

9   Internal Revenue Service. (2012, December 28). Questions and answers on employer shared responsibility provisions under the Affordable Care Act. Retrieved from http://www.irs.gov/uac/Newsroom/Questions-and-Answers-on-Employer-Shared-Responsibility-Provisions-Under-the-Affordable-Care-Act

GROUP BASIS

Large employer status must be calculated on a group basis.[10] A group basis means you can't separate one of your businesses and calculate it independently from the others. So, if you have a business with several locations, all those locations are calculated together to determine employer status.

Similarly, subsidiaries count towards your large employer status. If one company controls 80% or more of another company, then the FTs and FTEs of both companies are calculated together to determine large employer status. The same thing happens with an affiliated service, in which companies provide joint services to customers or other companies. Finally, controlled group businesses' FTs and FTEs are calculated together. If a group of 5 or fewer people own 80% of one company, or 50% of two or more companies, then those companies' FTs and FTEs are calculated together. These companies cannot be treated as individual businesses, but must all be grouped together as one when determining large employer status.

The second location (or second business, or second affiliated service) itself does not count as a separate business. Rather, it counts as part of a whole and must be calculated that way. This becomes more important for employers that own several businesses or have one business with several locations. In these cases, employers must take into account PT and FT employees for all of their businesses and locations.

If you think your company should be calculated on a group basis, please reference IRS section 1563(a) and contact your financial adviser. The controlled group rules are very

---

10   *Saraisky, S. (2013, May 10). Who is a large employer under Obamacare? Retrieved from http://www.jdsupra.com/legalnews/who-is-a-large-employer-under-obamacare-87331/*

complicated and we have only touched on them here.

Group Basis

LARGE EMPLOYER STATUS MUST BE CALCULATED
ON A GROUP BASIS

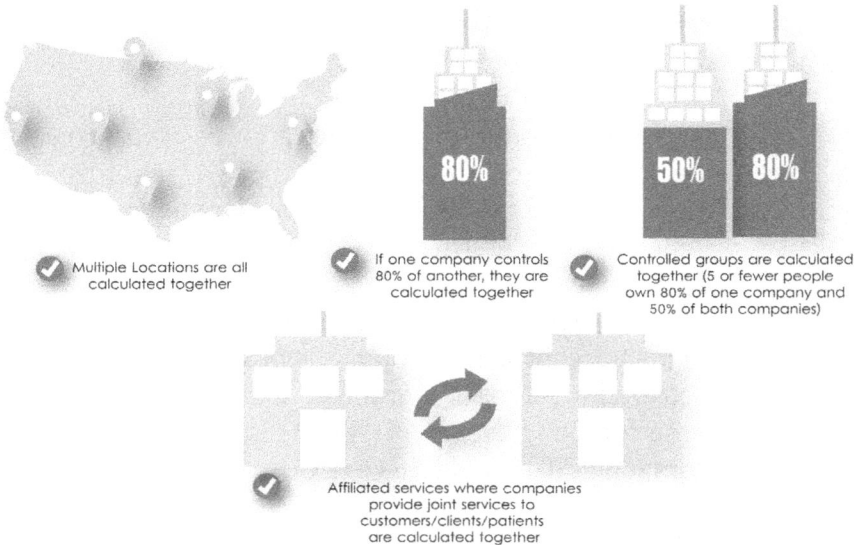

✓ Multiple Locations are all
calculated together

✓ If one company controls
80% of another, they are
calculated together

✓ Controlled groups are calculated
together (5 or fewer people
own 80% of one company and
50% of both companies)

✓ Affiliated services where companies
provide joint services to
customers/clients/patients
are calculated together

EMPLOYEES VS. INDEPENDENT CONTRACTORS: THE COMMON LAW TEST

The Common Law Test was devised by the IRS as a way for you to determine whether a worker is considered an employee or an independent contractor.[11] This is important because only employees are included in FT + FTE calculations;

---

11   *Internal Revenue Service. (2013, January 10). Independent contractor (self-employed) or employee? Retrieved from http://www.irs.gov/Businesses/Small-Businesses-&-Self-Employed/Independent-Contractor-%28Self-Employed%29-or-Employee%3F*

independent contractors are not.

Under the Common Law Test, a worker is considered your employee if you have the authority to direct and control the actions of that person while they are on the job. For example, can you determine what a worker is (or is not) allowed to do while at work/on the job?

The second consideration under the Common Law Test involves pay. An individual is an employee if you determine factors related to that individual's pay. For example, do you pay the worker and determine when the worker gets paid? Also, do you determine how a worker is reimbursed? An employee receives a paycheck at determined times, whereas a contractor may submit a bill for services provided.

Finally, you must consider your relationship with the worker under the Common Law Test. For example, do you have an ongoing contract with the worker? Do you provide the worker with ongoing benefits?

All three sets of questions (actions, money, and relationship) must be considered when determining whether an individual is an employee or an independent contractor. Answering "yes" to most of these questions would seem to indicate that the individual is an employee. Other times, some factors will indicate the individual is an employee and some will indicate the individual is an independent contractor. There is no set way to determine the status based on the answers given to the above questions. Instead, all the factors must be weighed together.

✅ Common Law Test

YOU ARE CONSIDERED AN EMPLOYEE IF:

The employer has the authority to direct and control your actions while on the job.

Contract?
Benefits?

The employer has a relationship with you through an ongoing contract and/or ongoing benefits.

Sun.	Mon.	Tues.	Wed.	Thurs.	Fri.	Sat.
14	15	16	17	18	19	20

Pay Day!

The employer can determine factors related to your individual pay. Does the employer determine when you get paid?

FOREIGN EMPLOYMENT

Foreign employment is not included in large employer calculations.[12] If you have employees outside of the US, those employees are not added to your total number of FT and FTE employees to determine whether you are a large employer. As a result, employers might decide to start exporting jobs outside of the US. Increasing foreign employment numbers could allow employers to avoid becoming large employers

---

12   Internal Revenue Service. (2012, December 28). Questions and answers on employer shared responsibility provisions under the Affordable Care Act. Retrieved from http://www.irs.gov/uac/Newsroom/Questions-and-Answers-on-Employer-Shared-Responsibility-Provisions-Under-the-Affordable-Care-Act

under Obamacare.

NEW EMPLOYERS

A new employer is an employer who did not exist the previous year. As a result, there were no employees to measure for the large employer calculation. It has been determined that if a new employer is expected to employ 50 or more FTs and FTEs, then that employer will be considered a large employer for that calendar year.[13]

SEASONAL EMPLOYEE EXEMPTION

If you employ a large number of seasonal employees, you may feel that it is unfair to include seasonal employees in the FT + FTE counts since those employees are only working for part of the year. The IRS took this into consideration while laying out the guidelines for determining large employer status and, if the two criteria below are met, you can exclude seasonal employees from your FT + FTE totals. A good faith interpretation of "seasonal" can be used until more clarification on the definition of seasonal is given.[14]

1. First, the seasonal employee must work less than 120 days in the year.[15] These 120 days do not have to be consecutive. If you have several employees that work for less than 120 total days throughout the year, you may be able to exclude them from your large employer calculations.

---

13   *Department of the Treasury. (2012, December 27). Shared responsibility for employers regarding health coverage. Retrieved from http://www.irs.gov/pub/ newsroom/reg-138006-12.pdf*
14   *Department of the Treasury. (2012, December 27). Shared responsibility for employers regarding health coverage. Retrieved from http://www.irs.gov/pub/ newsroom/reg-138006-12.pdf*
15   *Internal Revenue Service. (2011, May 23). Request for comments on shared responsibility for employers regarding health coverage (section 4980h). Retrieved from http://www.irs.gov/irb/2011-21_IRB/ar07.html*

2. Second, the count of FTs + FTEs cannot exceed 50 unless it does so **only** because of seasonal employees or you will be considered a large employer under Obamacare.[16] In other words, the sum of FTs and FTEs must be below 50 before adding the seasonal employees. If, at any time in the year, the FT + FTE sum is over 50 when there are no seasonal employees, then seasonal employees cannot be exempt from your large employer calculations.

If both of these criteria are met, then you can exclude seasonal employees from large employer calculations and potentially avoid being defined as a large employer under Obamacare.

---

16   *Internal Revenue Service. (2011, May 23). Request for comments on shared responsibility for employers regarding health coverage (section 4980h). Retrieved from http://www.irs.gov/irb/2011-21_IRB/ar07.html*

SEASONAL EMPLOYEE EXEMPTIONS

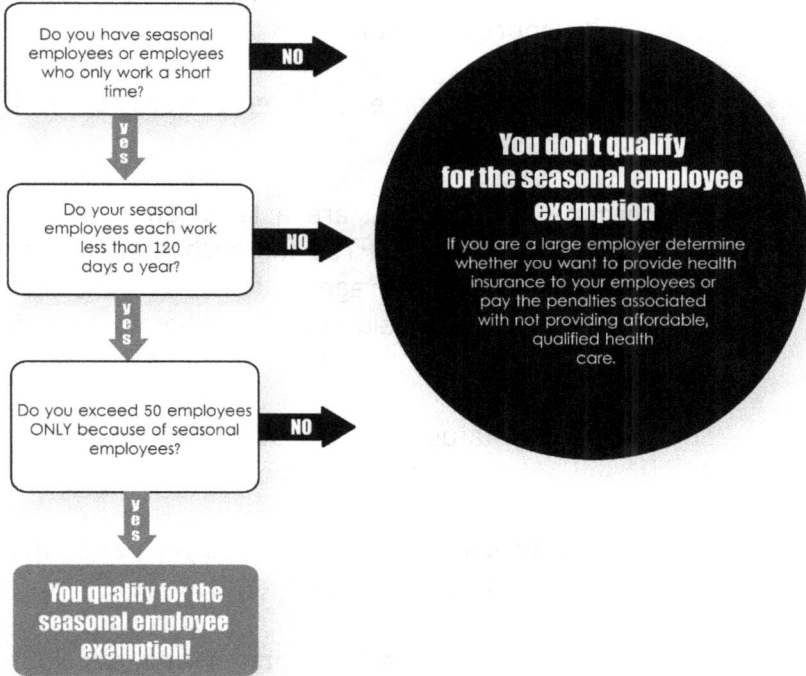

Do you have seasonal employees or employees who only work a short time?

NO →

yes ↓

Do your seasonal employees each work less than 120 days a year?

NO →

yes ↓

Do you exceed 50 employees ONLY because of seasonal employees?

NO →

yes ↓

You don't qualify for the seasonal employee exemption

If you are a large employer determine whether you want to provide health insurance to your employees or pay the penalties associated with not providing affordable, qualified health care.

You qualify for the seasonal employee exemption!

CHAPTER REVIEW

- You are a large employer if you employ 50 or more full-time (FT) employees and full-time equivalent employees (FTE).

- FT employees work at least an average of 30 hours a week or 130 hours a month.

- FTE represents part-time (PT) employees as a FT number.

- To determine whether you are a large employer, find your number of FTs and FTEs for each month of the previous year. Find the average for the year. If the result is 50 or more, you are considered a large employer under Obamacare.

- Large employer status must be calculated on a group basis (based on company ownership).

- To determine which workers are employees and which are contractors, use the IRS Common Law Test.

- Foreign employment is not counted when calculating large employer status.

- Seasonal employees may be excluded from large employer calculations if they work less than 120 days and if the inclusion of seasonal workers on the calculations reclassifies a small employer as a large employer.

3 — PENALTIES

OFFERING HEALTHCARE COVERAGE

To avoid penalties as a large employer, you must provide all FT employees and their dependents (but not spouses) insurance that meets two requirements.[1] First, the insurance must have minimum value coverage (discussed below). Second, the insurance must be affordable (also discussed below). If you wish to avoid receiving a penalty, you must make sure the insurance meets these two requirements and you must offer all eligible employees a chance to enroll in coverage once a year.

If you fail to meet those two requirements based on the current implementation of the law, you won't be penalized until at least one employee receives a premium tax credit to offset the cost of insurance. An employee receiving a premium tax credit is the trigger for the penalties. The amount of the penalties (discussed below) reflects this. If you do not offer insurance that is both affordable and has minimum value coverage, and no employee receives a premium tax credit, then you will not receive a penalty. These factors become

---

[1]   *Department of the Treasury. (2012, December 27). Shared responsibility for employers regarding health coverage. Retrieved from http://www.irs.gov/pub/ newsroom/reg-138006-12.pdf*

very important when deciding whether to offer insurance to employees ("Play") or to just pay the penalty ("Pay").

The IRS penalties are calculated on a monthly basis.[2] Therefore, one employee receiving a premium tax credit for one month will cause you to receive a penalty for one month. If you're a large employer and you don't offer coverage at all, you risk penalties every month that your employees receive a premium tax credit. However, if all your employees are offered coverage which meets the guidelines for most of the year (but not all of it), and some employees receive a premium tax credit for just a short period of time, you'll be liable for penalties for the months your employees received premium tax credits. Providing insurance for just most of the year will not protect you from penalties. If even one employee receives a premium tax credit to buy healthcare insurance, the IRS could assess a penalty against you for all FT employees if you aren't offering them coverage.

If an employee applies for and receives a premium tax credit for health coverage through an exchange, you will receive a notification from that exchange. This is likely going to be your only way of knowing whether you may later be penalized by the IRS for not offering minimum value and affordable coverage to that employee (and other employees). Remember, if you follow the rules and offer minimum value and affordable coverage, your employees will be ineligible for premium tax credits when purchasing through the exchange, so you shouldn't receive this notification. If you receive such a notification in error, you will want to start in the exchange appeals process.

---

2   *Internal Revenue Service. (2012, December 28). Questions and answers on employer shared responsibility provisions under the Affordable Care Act. Retrieved from http://www.irs.gov/uac/Newsroom/Questions-and-Answers-on-Employer-Shared-Responsibility-Provisions-Under-the-Affordable-Care-Act*

As you may be aware, the Obama administration delayed the penalties for employers during the year of 2014. This is primarily because the bureaucracy isn't fully prepared to handle notifications, assessments, penalties, and the underlying communications between the SHOPs, HHS, IRS, and other agencies. Expect for there to be roll out problems—there always are.

MINIMUM ESSENTIAL COVERAGE

Obamacare requires all Americans to carry health insurance with minimum essential coverage. In addition, if your business is classified as a large employer, you are required to offer minimum essential coverage to all FT employees.

A plan has minimum essential coverage, if the healthcare plan was obtained from one of the following:[3]

- An acceptable employer-sponsored program
- A health plan offered in the private market
- A grandfathered plan
- A government-sponsored program
    - Medicare
    - Medicaid
    - Some veteran plans
    - TRICARE
    - CHIP
    - Health plans for Peace Corps volunteers
    - Non-appropriated Fund Health Benefits Program of the Department of Defense

---

3   *Internal Revenue Service. (2013, January 30). Questions and answers on the individual shared responsibility provision. Retrieved from http://www.irs. gov/uac/Questions-and-Answers-on-the-Individual-Shared-Responsibility-Provision*

One goal of the minimum essential coverage (further explained in Chapter 9) is to minimize the number of fake or fraudulent claims against insurance policies, which will help offset the likely rise in insurance premiums that will be instituted by the insurance companies. Insurance companies will be responsible for paying additional taxes, such as the Transitional Reimbursement Program tax, and might pass on the costs of taxes to their customers.[4]

MINIMUM VALUE

Your healthcare coverage plan meets the minimum value if its "total allowed costs of benefits provided under the plan is less than 60 percent of the costs.[5]" This means that an average person in the population (employee) doesn't contribute more than 40% of the costs of insurance claims. Instead, the plan pays for 60% or more of the costs of insurance claims. These costs are estimated using the average cost of insurance claims for the an "average" person by using actuarial values.

MINIMUM VALUE OF

COVERAGE

Plan must have an actuarial value
of at least 60% (Bronze level or higher)

---

4   *Internal Revenue Service. (2012, November 30). ACA section 1341 transitional reinsurance program FAQs. Retrieved from http://www.irs.gov/uac/Newsroom/ACA-Section-1341-Transitional-Reinsurance-Program-FAQs*
5   *Internal Revenue Service. (2012, December 28). Questions and answers on employer shared responsibility provisions under the Affordable Care Act. Retrieved from http://www.irs.gov/uac/Newsroom/Questions-and-Answers-on-Employer-Shared-Responsibility-Provisions-Under-the-Affordable-Care-Act*

The IRS is still developing several methods to determine if an insurance plan has met the minimum value. Therefore, even though you will need to offer these plans to avoid certain penalties, the exact definitions are still somewhat ambiguous.

AFFORDABLE COVERAGE

A healthcare plan that is affordable is one in which premiums do not cost your employees more than 9.5% of the employee's household income.[6] This percentage may be adjusted in later years. If an employee's household income is $30,000 a year, the insurance cannot cost the employee more than 30,000 x .095, or $2,850 a year.

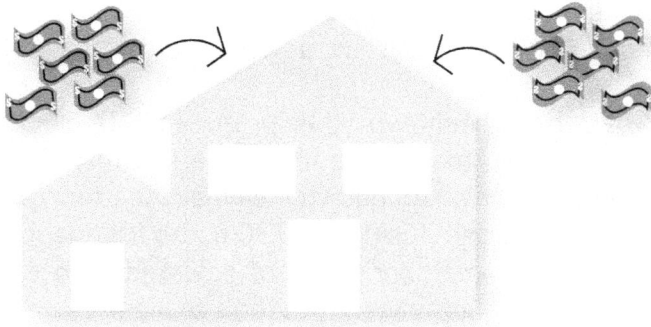

AFFORDABLE COVERAGE ≤ **9.5%** OF EMPLOYEE'S HOUSEHOLD INCOME

It may be difficult to determine your employee's household income when trying to ensure that healthcare coverage is affordable. The IRS created a safe harbor rule for you to determine whether healthcare coverage is affordable until at least January 1, 2015.[7] You can reference an employee's W-

---

6   *Internal Revenue Service. (2012, August 31). Determining full-time employees for purposes of shared responsibility for employers regarding health coverage (§ 4980h). Retrieved from http://www.irs.gov/pub/irs-drop/n-12-58.pdf*
7   *Internal Revenue Service. (2012, December 28). Questions and an-*

2 to determine household income. For the insurance plan to be affordable, its cost cannot exceed 9.5% of an employee's W-2 salary or wages. To use this safe harbor proactively, you will need to forecast what an employee's W-2 wages will be for the upcoming year and base contributions on that. Also, the employee's contribution must remain a consistent amount or percentage.[8] This will prevent you from offering affordable coverage and then raising the price over time.

The concept behind the affordability safe harbor is that an employee's household income could be greater than what is listed on the W-2. Therefore, the coverage has to be affordable because if the employee's household income is larger than what is stated on the W-2 and the employer has followed the safe harbor rule, then the cost of the health insurance plan is not above 9.5% of an employee's pay. If an employee waives coverage through the employer, the employer will not receive a penalty.

There have been two other proposed safe harbors that you could use to make sure insurance is affordable.[9] One uses the rate of pay. You determine what the employee should be paid for a month (using the 130 hours for one month), based on the staff member's rate of pay, and then compares the employee's monthly contribution to healthcare coverage to the monthly rate of pay. The employee's contribution cannot exceed 9.5% of the monthly rate of pay. Also, you cannot decrease the employee's pay rate during the year while using this method.

swers on employer shared responsibility provisions under the Affordable Care Act. Retrieved from http://www.irs.gov/uac/Newsroom/Questions-and-Answers-on-Employer-Shared-Responsibility-Provisions-Under-the-Affordable-Care-Act

8   ADP. (2013, March 19). Affordable Care Act (ACA) update series: Affordability safe harbor methods. Retrieved from http://www.adp.com/tools-and-resources/adp-research-institute/insights/insight-item-detail.aspx?id=6B5D32ED-B4CB-409E-AB47-69A800AEF83B

9   Department of the Treasury. (2012, December 27). Shared responsibility for employers regarding health coverage. Retrieved from http://www.irs.gov/pub/newsroom/reg-138006-12.pdf

You could also consider the Federal Poverty Line (FPL) when determining affordability. Individuals below 100% (138% in states that have expanded Medicaid) of the FPL are not eligible for a premium tax credit because they qualify for Medicaid. Therefore, if you set the cost of healthcare based at or below 100% (or 138% in states that have expanded Medicaid) of the FPL at the single rate, then you know that it will be affordable to all your employees.[10] The only people for whom it wouldn't be affordable would be those below 100% of the FPL, and those individuals will be eligible for Medicaid.

It is possible that insurance for a dependent could be considered unaffordable despite the insurance being calculated as affordable for the household. In these instances, the employee would be eligible for a premium tax credit. However, you are not penalized because the insurance was deemed affordable for the household.[11]

Note:

The IRS is the enforcement agency for all penalties relating to the Affordable Care Act.

The IRS and the HHS have created an affordability calculator and minimum value calculator. The calculators can be found on the regulation and guidance page for the Center for Consumer Information & Insurance Oversight (http://www.cms.gov/cciio/index.html).

---

10   *Department of the Treasury. (2012, December 27). Shared responsibility for employers regarding health coverage. Retrieved from http://www.irs.gov/pub/ newsroom/reg-138006-12.pdf*
11   *Internal Revenue Service. (2011, September 13). Request for comments on health coverage affordability safe harbor for employers. Retrieved from http:// www.irs.gov/pub/irs-drop/n-11-73.pdf*

COST OF PENALTIES

There are two types of penalties that an employer may receive: a penalty for not offering coverage to all FT employees (penalty A) and a penalty for offering coverage that is not of minimum value or affordable (penalty B). Each penalty is triggered when at least one employee receives a premium tax credit from an exchange. It is important to note that if you have employees who are ineligible for a premium tax credit (in other words, their income is more than 400% of the federal poverty line), then you will not receive a penalty for not offering insurance or insurance that does not meet Obamacare standards.

Penalty A (the penalty for not offering minimum essential healthcare coverage to all FT employees) is $2,000 times the number of full-time employees you have, minus 30, or $2,000 x (# FT employees - 30).[12] This penalty is triggered by employees receiving a premium tax credit to help them purchase coverage through an exchange. The IRS has accounted the possibility for errors in calculations and has proposed a 5% or 5 people (whichever is greater) buffer.[13] This means that only 95% of FT employees and their dependents must be offered healthcare coverage that meets the minimum value requirements and is affordable in order for the employer to avoid a penalty.[14] This buffer is not designed as a loophole for employers to avoid offering

---

12   The Henry J. Kaiser Family Foundation. (2011, March 25). Employer responsibility under the Affordable Care Act. Retrieved from http://kff.org/info-graphic/employer-responsibility-under-the-affordable-care-act/
13   Department of the Treasury. (2012, December 27). Shared responsibility for employers regarding health coverage. Retrieved from http://www.irs.gov/pub/newsroom/reg-138006-12.pdf
14   Internal Revenue Service. (2012, December 28). Questions and answers on employer shared responsibility provisions under the Affordable Care Act. Retrieved from http://www.irs.gov/uac/Newsroom/Questions-and-Answers-on-Employer-Shared-Responsibility-Provisions-Under-the-Affordable-Care-Act

insurance to all FT employees. Rather, it is a safety net in case a FT employee is overlooked and not offered coverage. So, if for some reason 5% of FT employees were overlooked and not offered coverage – or 5 people, whichever is greater – (maybe calculations to determine their status were incorrect), you may not be penalized. You should retain records of whether an employee declined offered coverage in order to avoid penalties from straying outside the 5% buffer from false claims that employees were not offered coverage.

You can receive penalty B for offering coverage that is not of minimum value and/or is not affordable. Similar to penalty A, penalty B is triggered when one employee receives a premium tax credit from an exchange to help purchase healthcare coverage. The penalty is $3,000 per FT employee who receives a premium tax credit.[15] The penalty amount is capped at the price of the first penalty, or $2,000 x (# FT employees – 30), so if you choose to "play" you won't pay more (in penalties at least) than if you had chosen to "Pay."

You may be safe from penalty A by offering coverage to 95% of FT employees. However, this does not make you safe from penalty B. An employee who was not offered coverage might receive a premium tax credit through an exchange if your offered coverage is not affordable or does not meet the minimum value. Penalty A is assessed with all FT employees who aren't offered coverage in mind. Penalty B is assessed for each employee who wasn't offered minimum value/ affordable coverage.

---

15   *The Henry J. Kaiser Family Foundation. (2011, March 25). Employer responsibility under the Affordable Care Act. Retrieved from http://kff.org/info-graphic/employer-responsibility-under-the-affordable-care-act/*

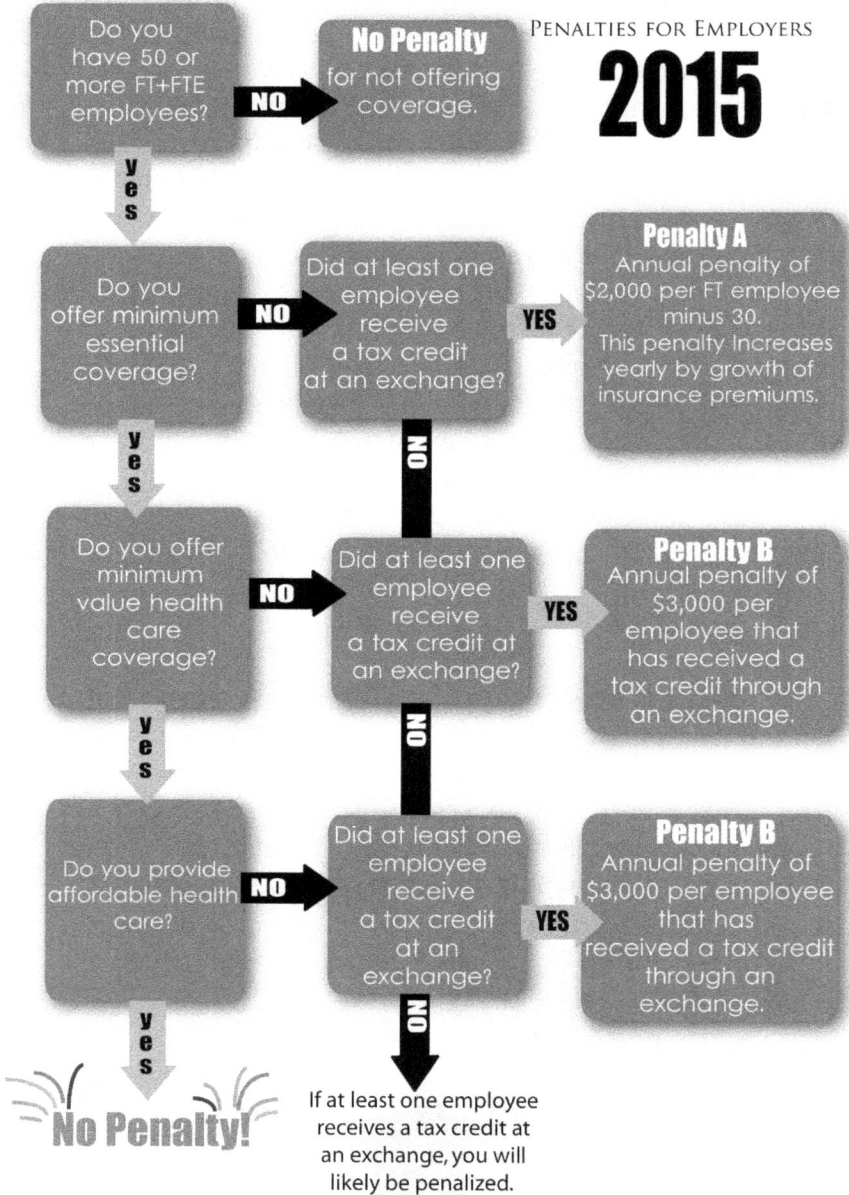

CALCULATING PENALTIES

If you meet all the requirements of healthcare coverage under Obamacare and some employees refuse that coverage, then those employees will not be eligible for a premium tax credit. Therefore, you will not be penalized.[16]

You are encouraged to have employees sign waivers if they or their dependents choose not to enroll in the insurance you offer. This will prevent employees from claiming that they were not offered the chance to enroll and will protect you from penalties. If waivers cannot be obtained, you should keep notes about employees who did not enroll and why there is no waiver on file. Keep in mind, employees who refuse the health insurance you offer that is at least minimum essential coverage, and is affordable, will not be eligible to receive an insurance premium tax credit through the exchange and will be penalized if they do not purchase insurance from either the exchange or the private market.

TRANSITIONAL RELIEF FOR FISCAL YEAR INSURANCE PLANS

The IRS recognizes that some healthcare coverage plans may not follow the calendar year. For these types of plans that were in existence before December 27, 2012, a transitional relief provision prevents employers from receiving penalties for the months in 2014 before the start of the 2015 healthcare coverage year.[17]

---

16   *The Henry J. Kaiser Family Foundation. (2011, March 25). Employer responsibility under the Affordable Care Act. Retrieved from http://kff.org/info-graphic/employer-responsibility-under-the-affordable-care-act/*
17   *Department of the Treasury. (2012, December 27). Shared responsibility for employers regarding health coverage. Retrieved from http://www.irs.gov/pub/newsroom/reg-138006-12.pdf*

PAYING PENALTIES

Note:

Remember, you can proactively dispute a penalty if you initiate the Exchange Appeals Process when the Exchange notifies you that an employee received a premium tax credit.

After your employees file their personal tax returns and you submit information about the healthcare coverage you offered, the IRS will contact you about any penalties accumulated over the past year.[18] You will then have a chance to dispute the penalties with the IRS.

If the IRS decides that the penalties are legitimate, then it will send you a notification detailing the amount owed and how to pay the penalty.[19]

PAY OR PLAY (AKA SHARED RESPONSIBILITY)

Obamacare's requirement that large businesses offer healthcare coverage to all FT employees is commonly referred to as "Shared Responsibility" or "Pay or Play." The second name refers to the decisions large employers make to either "pay" the penalty and not offer insurance to any FT

18   *Internal Revenue Service. (2012, December 28). Questions and answers on employer shared responsibility provisions under the Affordable Care Act. Retrieved from http://www.irs.gov/uac/Newsroom/Questions-and-Answers-on-Employer-Shared-Responsibility-Provisions-Under-the-Affordable-Care-Act*
19   *Internal Revenue Service. (2012, December 28). Questions and answers on employer shared responsibility provisions under the Affordable Care Act. Retrieved from http://www.irs.gov/uac/Newsroom/Questions-and-Answers-on-Employer-Shared-Responsibility-Provisions-Under-the-Affordable-Care-Act*

employees or only to some FT employees, or "play" and offer insurance that meets the minimum value and affordability requirements to all FT employees. You may choose to "pay" instead of "play" because the penalty may be more cost effective than offering affordable minimum value coverage to all FT employees.

There is no set method to determine whether pay or play is more advantageous. The pros and cons of each can only be decided on a case-by-case basis. What is your company's budget? Can you afford to pay the penalty? Can you afford to offer affordable minimum value insurance to all FT employees? Do you have existing health coverage plans? Do they qualify as grandfathered plans? Another important consideration is the fact that contributions to employees' healthcare costs are tax deductible. The penalties, however, are not.[20]

Will having health insurance reduce turnover, and increase retention? These questions and more must be considered when deciding to pay or play. Only you can decide which route to take after evaluating both of the options. There have been many predictions that you (an employer) will reduce the costs of paying or playing by reducing the number of FT employees that you have. This would lead to an increase in PT employees. Because the cost of penalties is based on FT employees, this would reduce the cost of paying. And, since you only have to provide coverage to FT employees, this would reduce the costs of playing. Reducing everyone's hours can look very appealing.

However, you should be aware that there can be some negative effects of converting staff to PT. PT employees are

---

20   *Department of the Treasury. (2012, December 27). Shared responsibility for employers regarding health coverage. Retrieved from http://www.irs.gov/pub/ newsroom/reg-138006-12.pdf*

more likely to leave a job than FT employees. Other companies offering benefits could cause those PT employees to leave even faster. You may not realize how expensive turnover is. In the restaurant industry, the average cost of turnover (per lost employee) is $2,000. If your turnover rates (and costs) increase because your employees aren't able to work as many hours as they need, converting everyone to PT to avoid penalties may not be cost-effective long term. You should also consider how PT employees can affect your business and make sure that your operations will still be able to run smoothly with a staff composed of more PT employees.

Another common prediction is the use of "skinny plans." These insurance plans offer bare-bones coverage that will be inexpensive for you. If you offer all FT employees a skinny plan, you won't receive Penalty A (you will not be penalized for not offering insurance to all FT employees and their dependents). However, some employees might still go to an exchange and get a premium tax credit to buy better insurance. Therefore, offering skinny plans would be betting that not many employees would end up going to an exchange.[21] As a result, the penalty would be much lower because it would be based only on those FT employees that went to the Exchange and received a premium tax credit, not all FT employees (penalty B).

---

21   *Roy, A. (2013, May 21). Employers can minimize their exposure to obamacare's penalties by offering low-cost 'skinny' coverage. Retrieved from http://www. forbes.com/sites/theapothecary/2013/05/21/employers-can-minimize-their-exposure-to-obamacares-health-insurance-mandate-by-offering-low-cost-skinny-coverage/*

CHAPTER REVIEW

- Large employers must offer health insurance that is affordable and of minimum value to all FT employees.

- You must offer minimum essential coverage to all FT employees.

- The IRS will allow you to overlook 5% of employees or 5 employees (whichever is greater) when offering healthcare coverage to FT employees without being penalized.

- The penalties are triggered when an employee receives a premium tax credit; penalty A (the penalty for not offering minimum essential coverage to all FT employees) is $2,000 x (# of FT - 30).

- You must offer minimum value coverage, which means the plan cannot pay less than 60% of healthcare expenses.

- You must offer affordable coverage, which means healthcare coverage does not cost more than 9.5% of the employee's household income.

- You can use their employee's W-2 to make sure that healthcare coverage is affordable.

- The penalties are triggered when an employee receives a premium tax credit; penalty B (the penalty for not affordable and/or minimum value coverage) is $3,000 x FT employees receiving a premium tax credit (cannot exceed $2,000 x (# of FT - 30)).

- Health plans which do not follow the calendar year will not receive penalties before the start of the 2014 healthcare year.

- The IRS will contact you about penalties after all employees have filed their individual tax returns.

- You must decide whether it is more profitable to "pay" the penalty and not offer insurance to all FT employees, or "play" and offer coverage that is affordable and of minimum value to all FT employees.

4 GUESS AND CHECK
MEASUREMENT METHOD

As the Obamacare legislation takes effect, it will require large employers to offer healthcare coverage to their full-time employees to avoid penalties. The IRS has determined these penalties will be assessed on a monthly basis. According to the law, the IRS will determine if an employee is full-time, and therefore entitled to healthcare coverage, using the number of hours the employee worked in a past month. The month is referred as a "look-back period". You may also use this method to determine an employee's status and healthcare eligibility.

However, this terminology is confusing because "look-back period" also refers to the period of time an employer uses to determine whether they are considered large or small employers (Chapter 2). Additionally, there are actually two methods to determine an employee's status and healthcare eligibility. The optional method, which was devised to eliminate the risk of underestimating the number of hours your employees will work in a month, and thereby incurring penalties, is referred to by many names. These include "look-back measurement method", "safe harbor method". The method itself is described in Chapter 5. Because of the confusing similarity of the terms, we will refer to the "look-back" method of determining an employee's full-time or part-time status and healthcare coverage eligibility as the "guess and check method".

Although the IRS has not acknowledged this name, it is apt to describe the method, because to apply it, you will need to "guess" the number of hours your employees will work each month, and "check" continuously for errors.

GUESS AND CHECK METHODS

If you decide not to use the lookback measurement method (covered in the next chapter) you will still have to determine which employees to offer affordable coverage to in order to avoid penalties. If you are using the "guess and check" method, you can retroactively determine FT and PT status on a month-to-month basis and offer coverage to those measured as FT the previous month. Or, you can proactively guess how many hours each employee will work for a month and offer coverage to FT employees based on that estimation. These methods have a greater risk factor than the IRS lookback measurement method. If an employee is overlooked or not offered coverage for a month when they were FT, you could receive penalties as you cannot purchase insurance retroactively.

The problem for guess and check calculations becomes obvious if an employee works 130 hours or more for the month, and you didn't offer health insurance. By the time the employee has worked enough hours to be FT, it is too late, and you will be penalized if you are a large employer. To help businesses accommodate this uncertainty, you can use the optional lookback measurement method covered in the next chapter.

CHAPTER REVIEW

- You can determine which employees to offer coverage to based on the number of hours each employee worked during the previous month.

- You can determine which employees to offer coverage to based on an estimate of the number of hours each employee will work for a month.

- The chance of receiving a penalty for not offering coverage to all FT employees is greater using the guess and check method instead of the lookback measurement method for determining employee status (Ch. 5).

5

THE IRS LOOKBACK
MEASUREMENT METHOD

As stated in Chapter 4, variable hour employees can work different shifts throughout the week, month, or year. If an employee is a variable hour employee, how do you determine whether they are PT or FT, and whether you need to offer health coverage? There are two methods for determining the status of an employee: the guess and check method, discussed in the previous chapter, and the lookback measurement method, which is explicitly defined by the IRS as an acceptable, but optional method.

WHAT IT IS

The IRS has developed a safe harbor, referred to as the lookback measurement method, to determine which employees are PT and which are FT under Obamacare. The lookback measurement method's purpose is to help you proactively determine which employees to offer health insurance to, so you can avoid a penalty. It establishes measurement periods to determine an employee's PT or FT status, and stability periods to establish how long an employee will be considered PT or FT (both of which are discussed below in more detail.) The use of the lookback measurement method is optional, but can help you figure out which employees are PT and which are FT.

If you decide to offer coverage to **all** of your employees, then the lookback measurement method is not needed because coverage is offered to everyone regardless of PT or FT status. Similarly, if you choose to pay the penalty and not offer insurance to FT employees, then you do not need to apply the lookback measurement method, because you will be opting to "pay" instead of "play."

MEASUREMENT PERIOD

The measurement period is the first period laid out by the lookback measurement method. As the name implies, its primary goal is measurement. It measures employee hours to determine whether an employee is PT or FT. Measuring hours under the lookback measurement period is similar to measuring hours while determining large employer status. The total number of hours for each week or month is totaled, and then the average is found. If that number is at or above 30 hours per week or 130 hours per month, the employee is considered FT and must be offered healthcare insurance under Obamacare. If affordable coverage that is of minimum value is not offered, you may be subject to a penalty.

Example:

Mark hires Jane on May 18th. The measurement period may begin on May 18th or June 1st. She works an average of 32 hours a week during the measurement period so she is considered a FT employee.

You can choose the length of the measurement period, but it must be between 3 and 12 months long. You can also choose when you want the standard measurement period (it will be the same year after year for employees) to start. For new hires, this period might start on the employee's hire date or the first day of the month after the hire date. The IRS does not explicitly state whether the start date for the measurement period needs to be the employee's hire date or the first of the month. Rather, the use of these two dates are guidelines. The first measurement period an employee is enrolled in is called the initial measurement period.

ADMINISTRATIVE PERIOD

The main purpose of the administrative period is to provide you with time to verify an employee's PT or FT status. Using the information gathered during the measurement period, you can determine which employees should be offered healthcare coverage. The administrative period also gives you time to enroll employees in insurance programs and perform other administrative duties associated with healthcare coverage. This period is optional. However, it provides you with an appropriate amount of time to perform the calculations. With the administration period, you don't have to worry about determining an employee's PT or FT status during the measurement period.

There are some rigid rules from the IRS about the proposed administrative period.

Example:

If Joan hires Bob on June 4, 2013, the combined measurement period and administrative period cannot extend beyond July 30th 2014.

- The administrative period must overlap the previous stability period so that the employee is never without healthcare coverage.
- The administrative period cannot be longer than 90

days.

- All dates between the hire date and the start of the measurement period and dates between the end of the measurement period and the beginning of the stability period (discussed below) are counted towards the 90 day limit.
    - In other words, all days immediately before and after the measurement period (that are not part of the stability period) are counted towards the 90 day administrative period limit.
- In addition to the 90 day length limitation, the administrative period and the initial measurement period together cannot last longer than the last day of the month after an employee's one year anniversary (or 13 months and some change).

STABILITY PERIOD

The purpose of the stability period is to lock in an employee's status as PT or FT. The determination of whether an employee is PT or FT is based on the measurement period. The status established by the measurement period lasts for the duration of the stability period, regardless of the hours worked during the stability period. So, if an employee measures as PT during the measurement period, that employee is considered PT for the entire stability period, even if the number of hours the employee works increases. Conversely, an employee who is measured as FT during the measurement period is considered FT for the entire stability period and must be offered health insurance, even if that employee's hours drop below 30 per week.

The measurement period is important because Obamacare requires you to offer healthcare coverage to all FT employees during the stability period in order to reduce the possibility of receiving a penalty. Therefore, you cannot reduce those hours to avoid having to offer insurance. Even if the hours are reduced, insurance still has to be offered until the stability period has ended.

The stability period can get tricky when dealing with new employees and there are a couple of guidelines when it comes to determining their stability periods. If an employee is considered FT after the initial measurement period, then the associated stability period cannot be shorter than the initial measurement period and must be at least 6 months.

If the employee is not measured as FT during the initial measurement period, then the associated stability period can be only one month longer than the initial measurement period.

Example:

Joe's Flowers decides on an initial measurement period of 4 months and an administrative period of 1 month. Their stability period should be no longer than 5 months.

In addition, the stability period cannot last longer than the remainder standard measurement period plus the standard administrative period. This allows you to use a 12 month stability period and gives you some flexibility when hiring new employees. To meet the requirement that the initial measurement period and administrative period do not last longer than the last day of the 13th or 14th month of the individual's employment, the employer can choose an initial measurement period of 11 months instead of twelve.

REVIEW OF THE LOOKBACK MEASUREMENT PERIOD METHOD

The measurement period is used to determine whether an employee is PT or FT. It can last anywhere between 3 and 12 months.

The administrative period is optional, but provides you with a chance to review employees' hours, determine whether they are PT or FT, and enroll them in healthcare coverage if need be. It cannot last longer than 90 days.

The stability period locks in an employee's PT or FT status, despite the number of hours worked. Therefore, it gives you a set period of time during which to offer employees coverage. This is especially helpful if an employee's hours change from month to month, making it hard to determine whether they are PT or FT.

Safe Harbor Periods For Determining Employee Status

Legend	
○	Administrative Period
●	Measurement Period
○	Stability Period

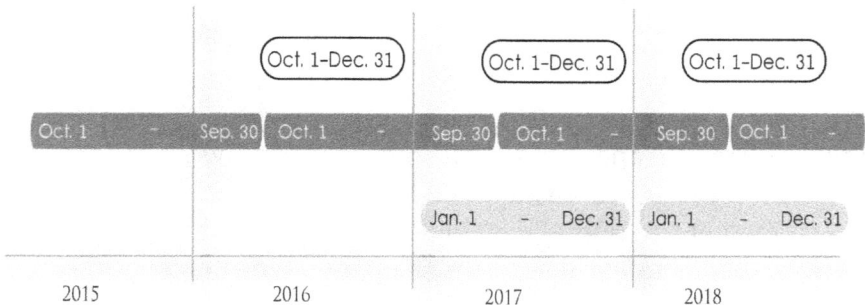

Oct. 1–Dec. 31		Oct. 1–Dec. 31		Oct. 1–Dec. 31	

| Oct. 1 | – | Sep. 30 | Oct. 1 | – | Sep. 30 | Oct. 1 | – | Sep. 30 | Oct. 1 | – |

| | Jan. 1 | – | Dec. 31 | Jan. 1 | – | Dec. 31 |

| 2015 | 2016 | 2017 | 2018 |

The periods are continuous. Therefore, a measurement period always occurs while an employee is in a stability period. This enables the employee to always be in a stability period and be offered healthcare coverage if necessary.

ONGOING EMPLOYEES

An ongoing employee is one who has been employed for one standard measurement period or more. Ongoing employees are measured differently than newly-hired employees. Set periods are established to be used year after year for these employees. As a result, there are standard periods that can be used for all employees so that you don't have to track several different measurement and stability periods. The set periods can only be changed for years that do not change an employee's measurement period or their corresponding stability period. For example, if an employee is in a measurement period for the year 2013, the length of that period cannot change because it will affect the corresponding stability period in 2014.

You can use different period lengths and dates for different categories of employees. These categories are:

- Union vs. non-union
- Different bargaining agreements
- Salaried vs. hourly
- Employees in different states

Unpaid leave, including jury duty and FMLA leave, must be included in the measurement period for ongoing employees. There are two different ways to account for this. You can find the average hours worked for the time period that the employee is at work and apply that average to the entire measurement period. Or, you can apply the normal number of hours the employee is supposed to work to the period of time off. Both of these methods will account for unpaid leave.

Example Safe Harbor Periods for ONGOING EMPLOYEES

Legend

- ● Measurement Period
- ○ Administrative Period
- ○ Stablility Period

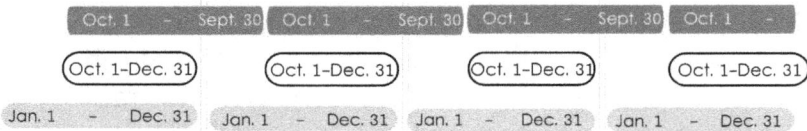

Oct. 1 – Sept. 30	Oct. 1 – Sept. 30	Oct. 1 – Sept. 30	Oct. 1 –
Oct. 1–Dec. 31	Oct. 1–Dec. 31	Oct. 1–Dec. 31	Oct. 1–Dec. 31
Jan. 1 – Dec. 31	Jan. 1 – Dec. 31	Jan. 1 – Dec. 31	Jan. 1 – Dec. 31

NEW EMPLOYEES

A new employee is any employee that has not been employed for at least as long as one standard measurement period. In other words, a new hire. In some cases, the lookback measurement method isn't needed to determine if a new hire is PT or FT. For example, if a new employee is expected to work at least 30 hours per week, then that employee is considered FT. The lookback measurement method isn't necessary because you already know the employee's status.

Many seasonal employees and variable hour employees, it can be difficult at the time of hire. In these cases, the lookback measurement method periods are handy for determining status and deciding who should be offered healthcare coverage. Without the lookback measurement method, you would have to determine an employee's eligibility for healthcare coverage on a monthly basis. This can become very time consuming if an employee's hours are constantly changing. There is also a greater chance that there will be mistakes in the calculations because they are done so often. Calculations would have to be made each month and the potential status changes could alter whether that employee should be offered healthcare coverage under Obamacare from month to month. In contrast, the lookback measurement method allows you to establish a set period of time for which an employee's status, and therefore the requirement to be enrolled in healthcare coverage, does not change. It also protects you from being penalized for not offering coverage during a month because the employee's status was still under determination.

You cannot decide that a new non-seasonal employee is a variable hour employee simply because you expect to fire that employee before the end of the initial measurement period. In other words, you cannot hire an employee to work full-time hours and avoid offering them coverage by putting them in an initial measurement period because you know they will not last the entire period (the expectation being that the average across the entire measurement period won't be 30 hours a week). Transitional guidance will delay this regulation until January 1, 2015.

Similarly, if a PT employee is promoted during the initial measurement period in such a way that he would have been measured as FT if he had been hired in that promoted position, then you are required to offer healthcare coverage to that employee. You must offer coverage on the 1st day of the fourth month after the employee's promotion. Or, if the employee is finally measured as a FT employee, then coverage must be offered on the 1st day of the month after the initial measurement (and optional administrative) period.

Employees are not eligible for minimum essential coverage (see Ch. 3) if you do not offer healthcare coverage. The times during which you do not offer health insurance could include the measurement and administrative periods before coverage is offered to an employee. Because employees are not eligible for minimum essential coverage, they could potentially receive a premium tax credit at a federal or state Exchange. The IRS hasn't been clear on whether you will be penalized. Please consult your insurance broker and expect updates from the IRS. For additional updates, you can also visit our website www.employersandobamacare.com.

You can use a waiting period of no more than 90 calendar days before enrolling employees in health coverage. This period includes weekends, holidays, and paid time off. Otherwise, you could be penalized. Your policies should address whether or not an employee's waiting period restarts if that employee misses a day of work during the waiting period. However, paid time off will not cause the waiting period to restart. Employees in the waiting period will not be penalized for not having insurance as long as their employer's insurance is affordable and meets the minimum value requirements.

Example Safe Harbor Periods for
New Employees

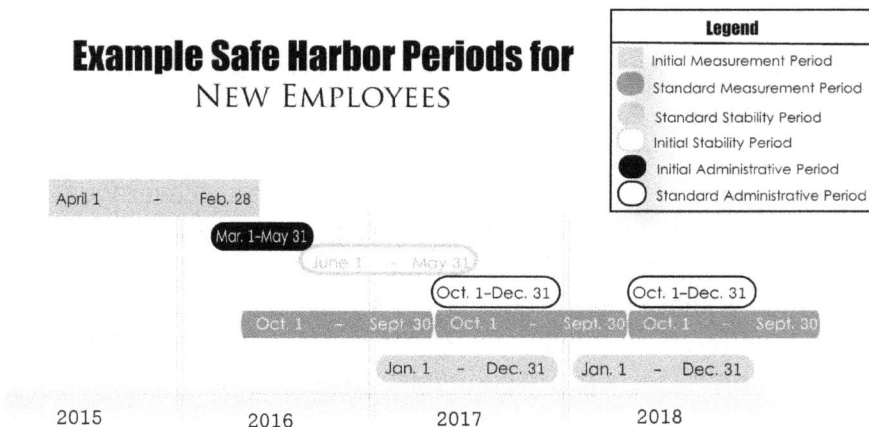

Legend	
	Initial Measurement Period
	Standard Measurement Period
	Standard Stability Period
	Initial Stability Period
	Initial Administrative Period
	Standard Administrative Period

April 1 – Feb. 28
Mar. 1–May 31
June 1 – May 31
Oct. 1–Dec. 31   Oct. 1–Dec. 31
Oct. 1 – Sept. 30   Oct. 1 – Sept. 30   Oct. 1 – Sept. 30
Jan. 1 – Dec. 31   Jan. 1 – Dec. 31

2015   2016   2017   2018

RE-HIRED EMPLOYEES

What happens when an employee leaves a company (for example, unpaid leave), and then returns to that same company? Under the lookback measurement method, some employees will be considered ongoing employees and some will be considered new employees. Employees who are re-hired or returning from unpaid leave who have not worked for 26 weeks (or more) are considered new employees. However, if they have worked 26 weeks or more, they are considered ongoing employees.

You can also choose to use the rule of parity when determining if a returning employee is an ongoing employee or a new hire. This rule states that if the employee has been absent from work for more than 4 weeks, and the amount of time gone is longer than the length of employment before being absent from work, then that employee can be considered a new employee.

This will affect your decision about whether the re-hire should be placed in an initial measurement period or in the standard measurement period with the rest of the employees.

CONVERTING NEW EMPLOYEES TO ONGOING EMPLOYEES

How do you transition those new hires to the standard measurement period along with the other ongoing employees?

When the new hire's initial periods overlap the standard measurement period (used for ongoing employees), enroll the new hire in that standard measurement period. This will result in an employee's initial periods overlapping the standard periods. The overlapping periods will get new hires on track with the other ongoing employees so that everyone is using the standard periods.

The overlapping periods could have two potential effects on an employee's PT or FT status:

If an employee is measured as FT during the initial measurement period, then that employee is considered FT for the corresponding stability period. This FT status continues even if the employee is then measured as PT during the standard measurement period while in the initial stability period. That employee is still considered FT for the entire length of the stability period associated with the initial measurement period and does not become PT until the end of the initial stability period. In this case, the employee must be offered insurance if you wish to avoid penalties.

Conversely, if an employee is measured as PT during the initial measurement period, but FT during the standard measurement period, the employee transitions to FT for the standard stability period, even if the employee is still in the initial stability period.

WHAT ABOUT 2014?

If you decide to use the lookback measurement method, you will need to begin your measurement period in 2014. That way, your stability starts in 2015 and you can easily track who should be offered coverage in order to avoid receiving a penalty. A transitional rule exists for those wishing to use a one-year measurement and stability period. For 2013 only, you can use a measurement period of less than a year (but more than 3 months) and a corresponding stability period of one year, and it must end no more than 90 days before the start of the plan year in 2014. That means if you want to use a stability period of a year, you need to start your measurement period on or before July 1, 2013.

CHAPTER REVIEW

- The IRS has established a safe harbor called the lookback measurement method that employers can use to determine which employees are considered FT.

- The measurement period is used to determine whether an employee is PT or FT.

- The administrative period is used to verify the employee status and enroll employees in healthcare coverage.

- The stability period locks in the employee's status as PT or FT.

- Ongoing employees have set measurement, administrative, and stability periods.

- If you use the lookback measurement method, your measurement period will need to start in 2013 so that the stability period and healthcare coverage start in 2014.

6

EMPLOYEE
NOTIFICATIONS

Under Obamacare, you will be required to notify your employees about certain aspects of healthcare coverage. If you do not comply with any of these new notification requirements, you will be subject to significant, varying fees and penalties. These are assigned for every day you fail to disburse the notifications to your employees.

EXPLANATION AND NOTIFICATION OF EXCHANGES

The Fair Labor Standards Act requires that you inform employees about federal and state exchanges by October 1, 2013. New employees should receive the notification when they are hired. The notification needs to contain the following information:[1]

- The existence of exchanges
- Exchange services
- How to contact exchanges
- How to receive a premium tax credit when an employer's plan does meet the minimum value and affordability

---

1   The Center for Consumer Information & Insurance Oversight. (2013, January 24). Affordable Care Act implementation FAQs - set 11. Retrieved from http://cciio.cms.gov/resources/factsheets/aca_implementation_faqs11.html

requirements
- The fact that an employee may not be eligible for employer healthcare contributions if that employee receives insurance through an exchange
- The fact that employer healthcare contributions may not count towards income in regards to income taxes

The Department of Labor has released a model of this notification (one each for employers that offer insurance and employers that don't offer insurance). This form (OMB Form 1210-0149) is also available on our website www.EmployersAndObamacare.com.

HEALTHCARE COVERAGE INFORMATION

If you are a large employer and you offer healthcare coverage to your employees, you must provide them with a notification that contains the following information pertaining to coverage for the previous year by January 31:[2]

- Employer's name
- Employer's address
- Employer's contact information (including phone number)
- Offered healthcare coverage details

AUTOMATIC ENROLLMENT NOTICE

If you have over 200 employees, then you must automatically enroll FT employees in healthcare coverage.[3] You have the

---

2   *Internal Revenue Service. (2012, May 14). Request for comments on reporting by applicable large employers on health insurance coverage under employer-sponsored plans. Retrieved from http://www.irs.gov/irb/2012-20_IRB/ar10. html*

3   *United Healthcare Services, INC. (2012, February 23). Summary of Benefits and Coverage and the Uniform Glossary. Retrieved from http://www.uhc.*

right to choose the healthcare coverage plan for auto-enrollment. You will be required to notify employees of the automatic enrollment and inform them that they can choose to opt out of coverage.[4] Because this requirement has been delayed for an unspecified amount of time, you don't have to distribute these notifications now, but be aware of them so that you are prepared to give them out when the delay ends.

SUMMARY OF BENEFITS AND COVERAGE NOTIFICATION

You will be required to give your employees a Summary of Benefits and Coverage (SBC) statement detailing the specifics of the offered coverage. The information in this statement must include:[5]

- Coverage information and examples (scenarios for different medical problems)
- Cost-sharing information (deductible, co-pay, co-insurance)
- Limits, omissions, or decreases in coverage
- Guideline to renew coverage
- Explanation that the SBC is only a summary
- Insurance company's contact information for questions
- Internet site where the plan's information can be reviewed
- Information to access the Uniform Glossary (which defines terms used in reference to healthcare insurance) and the

---

com/united_for_reform_resource_center/health_reform_provisions/summary_of_benefits_and_coverage.htm

4 *Internal Revenue Service. (2012, January 1). Frequently asked questions from employers regarding automatic enrollment, employer shared responsibility, and waiting periods. Retrieved from http://www.irs.gov/pub/irs-drop/n-12-17.pdf*

5 *United Healthcare Services, INC. (2012, February 23). Summary of Benefits and Coverage and the Uniform Glossary. Retrieved from http://www.uhc.com/united_for_reform_resource_center/health_reform_provisions/summary_of_benefits_and_coverage.htm*

Affordable Care Act

OTHER EMPLOYEE NOTIFICATIONS

In addition to the above-mentioned notifications, you will be required to distribute notifications detailing the following specifics.

- Grandfathered status and benefits[6]
- A 30-day written notice of proposed cancellation of coverage[7]
- A 60-day notification of any material modification in coverage[8]

6   *Internal Revenue Service. (2012, August 2). National taxpayer advocate testimony on Affordable Care Act. Retrieved from http://www.irs.gov/pub/irs-utl/ testimony_house_oversight_aca_080212.pdf*
7   *Internal Revenue Service. (2010, June 28). Requirements for group health plans and health insurance issuers under the Patient Protection and Afford-able Care Act relating to preexisting condition exclusions, lifetime and annual limits, rescissions, and patient protections. Retrieved from http://www.gpo.gov/fdsys/pkg/ FR-2010-06-28/pdf/2010-15277.pdf*
8   *United Healthcare Services, INC. (2012, February 23). Summary of Benefits and Coverage and the Uniform Glossary. Retrieved from http://www.uhc. com/united_for_reform_resource_center/health_reform_provisions/summary_of_ benefits_and_coverage.htm*

CHAPTER REVIEW

- You need to provide employees with information about their healthcare coverage.

- You need to provide employees with information about the exchanges.

- If you have more than 200 employees you will need to notify employees about automatic enrollment in insurance (delayed).

- You need to provide employees with a Summary of Benefits and Coverage notification.

7

REPORTING TO AGENCIES

You will be required to report certain information about healthcare coverage to government agencies.

IRS REPORTING

Beginning in 2015, if you provide health insurance to your employees, you must report the specifics of the offered coverage to the IRS.[1] This notification must include the following information:[2]

- Employer name, identification number, and contact information
- Date of the notification
- Determination of whether coverage offered is of minimum value and affordable:
    - Length of waiting period
    - Months for which coverage was offered
    - Least expensive option's premium (for each category)
    - The amount of the employer's contribution

---

1   *Internal Revenue Service. (2013, July 9). Notice 2013-45. Retrieved from http://www.irs.gov/pub/irs-drop/n-13-45.PDF*
2   *Internal Revenue Service. (2012, May 14). Request for comments on reporting by applicable large employers on health insurance coverage under employer-sponsored plans. Retrieved from http://www.irs.gov/irb/2012-20_IRB/ar10.html*

toward the cost of benefits
- Number of FT employees working for the employer each month
- For each employee:
    - Name
    - Address
    - Taxpayer identification number
    - Months of coverage under plan (for employee and dependents)

W-2 REPORTING

Beginning in 2013, if you have more than 250 W-2s, you will be required by the IRS to report the cost of employer healthcare coverage on each employee's W-2.[3] The exact specifications of what must be reported have not yet been determined. However, the IRS has set some specifications when it comes to W-2 reporting.[4] By reporting this information on the annual W-2 form, you are providing employees and the government information about the cost of the healthcare coverage.[5]

Additionally, self-insured employers must report healthcare coverage enrollment information to the IRS. The consequences to businesses that fail to follow the reporting procedures are still unclear at this time. Continue to watch for updates on our website:
www.EmployersAndObamacare.com.

---

3   Ernst & Young. (2012, September). The Affordable Care Act: Are companies ready to meet the requirements? Retrieved from http://www.ey.com/US/en/Issues/Governance-and-reporting/Audit-Committee/BoardMatters-Quarterly--September-2012---4---The-Affordable-Care-Act
4   United Healthcare Services, INC. (2012, January 25). W-2 reporting. Retrieved from http://www.uhc.com/united_for_reform_resource_center/health_reform_provisions/w_2_reporting.htm
5   Internal Revenue Service. (2012, January 1). Interim guidance on informational reporting to employees of the cost of their group health insurance coverage. Retrieved from http://www.irs.gov/pub/irs-drop/n-12-09.pdf

CHAPTER REVIEW

- You have to provide the IRS with information about healthcare coverage offered.

- You have to report healthcare costs on employees' W-2s if you issue more than 250 W-2's in a given year.

PART 2:
INDIVIDUALS AND
SMALL BUSINESSES

8
INDIVIDUALS AND SMALL BUSINESSES

OBAMACARE REGULATIONS

Certain aspects of Obamacare pertain to individuals rather than businesses. Still, you will need to be prepared to act as a resource to your employees as they navigate the individual mandate. This is particularly true if you opt to not offer healthcare coverage.

Keep in mind that you will be responsible for finding healthcare for yourself that complies with the Obamacare regulations. If you as an individual don't have Obamacare compliant health insurance, you'll get taxed. The same rule is true for your employees.

INDIVIDUAL PREMIUM TAX CREDITS

Some individuals may be eligible for a premium tax credit to help pay for healthcare coverage.[1] This premium tax credit is based on the Silver plan (Ch. 10).[2] Many experts believe

---

[1]   HHS Office of the Assistant Secretary for Planning and Evaluation. (2012, April). The Affordable Care Act: Coverage implications and issues for immigrant families. Retrieved from http://aspe.hhs.gov/hsp/11/ImmigrantAccess/Coverage/ib.shtml
[2]   The Henry J. Kaiser Family Foundation. (2011, April 17). What the actuarial values in the Affordable Care Act mean. Retrieved from http://kaiserfamilyfoundation.files.wordpress.com/2013/01/8177.pdf

Note:

A Silver Plan covers 70% of medical expenses and the insured pays 30% out of pocket.

A Bronze Plan covers 60% of medical expenses and the insured pays 40% out of pocket.

that those who receive premium tax credits can still enroll in a Bronze plan and that the part of the premium tax credit not applied to the cost of the plan can be used to offset premium overages or out of pocket costs.

If an individual refuses healthcare coverage from an employer offering coverage that meets the minimum value and affordability requirements (Ch. 3), then that individual will not be eligible for a premium tax credit.[3] Similarly, individuals who buy insurance in the private market are not eligible for a premium tax credit. Premium tax credits are only available to those who buy healthcare coverage through an exchange and did not opt out of their employer's offered affordable coverage.[4]

Under the terms of Obamacare, individuals with an income level between 100% and 400% of the federal poverty line may be eligible for a premium tax credit. Individuals are only eligible if they do not receive Medicare or Medicaid benefits, or their employer doesn't offer affordable minimum value healthcare coverage.

---

3   *Internal Revenue Service. (2012, July 30). Minimum value of an employer-sponsored health plan. Retrieved from http://www.irs.gov/pub/irs-drop/n-12-31.pdf*
4   *Internal Revenue Service. (2012, July 30). Minimum value of an employer-sponsored health plan. Retrieved from http://www.irs.gov/pub/irs-drop/n-12-31.pdf*

INDIVIDUAL TAX PENALTIES

If an individual chooses to opt out of buying health insurance, she may have to pay a tax for the months that she and her dependents do not have coverage. This tax was deemed constitutional by the Supreme Court in 2012 as a tax for not purchasing insurance. The justification for this ruling is that the nation has the power to tax its citizens. This remains a controversial topic despite the Supreme Court's ruling.

The individual shared responsibility tax penalties begin January 1, 2014.[5] There is a grace period during which an individual can be without coverage for no more than three months and not be taxed. However, that period must only occur no more than once a year. An individual who does not have health insurance will receive a tax, which will be pro-rated to reflect the number of months that the individual was without healthcare coverage.[6] The tax penalties are listed below:

- (2014) $95 per adult and $47.50 per child (up to $285 per family) or 1.0% of family income, whichever is greater
- (2015) $325 per adult and $162.50 per child (up to $975 per family) or 2.0% of family income, whichever is greater
- (2016) $695 per adult and $347.50 per child (up to $2,085 per family) or 3.0% of family income, whichever is greater

After 2016, the tax will adjust based on the cost of living. The IRS has not put forth any information regarding how the

---

5   *The Henry J. Kaiser Family Foundation. (2013, May 2). The requirement to buy coverage under the Affordable Care Act. Retrieved from http://kff.org/info-graphic/the-requirement-to-buy-coverage-under-the-affordable-care-act/*
6   *The Henry J. Kaiser Family Foundation. (2013, May 2). The requirement to buy coverage under the Affordable Care Act. Retrieved from http://kff.org/info-graphic/the-requirement-to-buy-coverage-under-the-affordable-care-act/*

taxes could change in coming years.

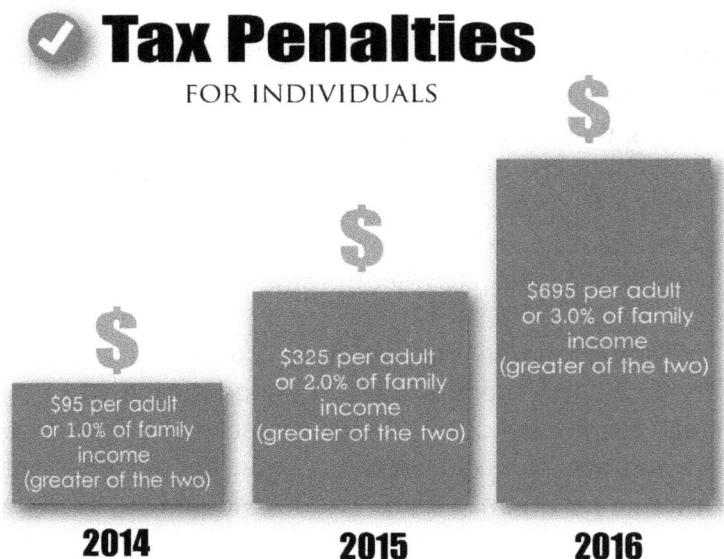

✅ Tax Penalties

FOR INDIVIDUALS

$

$

$95 per adult
or 1.0% of family
income
(greater of the two)

$325 per adult
or 2.0% of family
income
(greater of the two)

$695 per adult
or 3.0% of family
income
(greater of the two)

2014   **2015**   **2016**

For example, if an individual has a household income of $50,000, the percentage would be 1% of the difference between $50,000 and the tax threshold (which was $9,350 for an individual in 2010). Assuming the tax threshold is $10,000 in 2014, a percentage penalty for this employee would be $400. Because this percentage penalty is greater than the flat dollar penalty for 2014 (which is $95), he would pay the percentage penalty ($400).

To be exempt from a tax for not having insurance, the individual must qualify for at least one of the following exemptions:[7]

- Being part of a religion that does not accept healthcare

---

7   The Henry J. Kaiser Family Foundation. (2013, May 2). The requirement to buy coverage under the Affordable Care Act. Retrieved from http://kff.org/info-graphic/the-requirement-to-buy-coverage-under-the-affordable-care-act/

- Incarceration
- Being an undocumented immigrant
- Being a member of an Indian Tribe
- Individual income is low enough not to file a tax return
- Family income is low enough that no tax return is filed
- Using 8% of income to pay for healthcare coverage, not including employer contributions and tax credits

You should be aware of these requirements and taxes because it may affect employers as well as their employees. Not only will employees be interested in this information, but if you choose not to offer healthcare coverage at your company, you will be responsible for buying coverage for yourself that meets the above standards. Otherwise, you may receive a tax for any months during which you did not have insurance.

SMALL EMPLOYER TAX CREDIT

An employer with fewer than 50 full-time and full-time equivalent employees is not required to provide healthcare coverage to full-time employees. However, providing insurance to employees can be beneficial. It provides an incentive for potential applicants to apply to your business because offering benefits can make you more attractive than your competition. Additionally, coverage helps build employee morale because employees will feel that you have their well-being in mind. Also, employees will not need to worry and stress about finding insurance coverage because you are taking care of them.

Small businesses with less than 25 full-time equivalent employees that offer healthcare coverage to employees may be eligible for a tax credit to help pay for health insurance if insurance is purchased through the Small Business

Health Options Program (Ch.9).[8] The calculations used for determining eligibility for the small employer tax credit are different from calculating FTEs for large employer status, so do not confuse the two calculations. Calculations should include paid-time off and exclude business owners, business partners, their family members, and all seasonal employees that work less than 120 days in the year.[9] IRS Form 8941 is intended to help you with these calculations, but we've laid out the basics below.

To calculate whether you qualify for a small employer tax credit:[10]

1. For each employee, determine the total hours that he or she worked for the year, including paid time off, capping each employee at 2,080 hours. If an employee worked more than 2,080 hours, just record 2,080 for that employee.
2. Add up all of your employees' total hours worked for the year.
3. Divide that total by 2,080. If the result includes a decimal, round down.
4. If the result is less than 25, you may qualify (depending on the information in the next paragraph) for a small employer tax credit. However, if the result is more than 10, your tax credit percentage may be reduced.[11]

In order to qualify for this tax credit, the employees must

8   HealthCare.gov. (2013, June 21). What is the SHOP marketplace? Retrieved from https://www.healthcare.gov/what-is-the-shop-marketplace
9   Internal Revenue Service. (2013, January 24). Small business healthcare tax credit questions and answers: Determining FTEs and average annual wages. Retrieved from http://www.irs.gov/uac/Small-Business-Health-Care-Tax-Credit-Questions-and-Answers:-Determining-FTEs-and-Average-Annual-Wages
10   Internal Revenue Service. (2013, January 24). Small business healthcare tax credit questions and answers: Determining FTEs and average annual wages. Retrieved from http://www.irs.gov/uac/Small-Business-Health-Care-Tax-Credit-Questions-and-Answers:-Determining-FTEs-and-Average-Annual-Wages
11   Internal Revenue Service. (2010, December 5). Instructions for Form 8941. Retrieved from http://www.irs.gov/pub/irs-pdf/i8941.pdf

be paid an average annual salary of less than $50,000. To determine the average salary of your employees, add up all of their salaries (excluding the owners, family members, and seasonal employees that work less than 120 days a year) and divide by the number of FTEs you have. If that number is less than $50,000 you may qualify for the tax credit. However, if it is greater than $25,000, your tax credit percentage may be reduced.[12]

YOUR BUSINESS IS ELIGIBLE FOR A TAX CREDIT IF:

You have less than 25 FTE employees & Your employees' average salaries are below $50,000 & You provide health insurance that covers at least 50% of the premium costs of health insurance based on the single rate

Another requirement for the tax credit is that you must provide health insurance that covers at least 50% of the premium costs based on the individual rate.[13] The amount covered must be the same for each employee. In other words, 50% of premium costs can't be covered for Employee A while 70% of premium costs are covered for Employee B.

You can use IRS Form 8941 to determine the amount of the tax credit you will receive. The credit is then claimed

---

12   Internal Revenue Service. (2010, December 5). Instructions for Form 8941. Retrieved from http://www.irs.gov/pub/irs-pdf/i8941.pdf

13   Internal Revenue Service. (2012, September 26). Small business health-care tax credit for small employers. Retrieved from http://www.irs.gov/uac/Small-Business-Health-Care-Tax-Credit-for-Small-Employers

as business credit on tax returns.[14] For tax-exempt small businesses, the tax credit is a refundable tax credit.[15]

For 2013, the tax credit is up to 35% of insurance costs for small businesses and up to 25% of insurance costs for small non-profit organizations.[16] The tax credit is expected to increase for 2014 to a maximum of 50% of insurance costs for small businesses and a maximum of 35% of insurance costs for small non-profit organizations. The credit is intended to make the cost of providing insurance much lower, and incentivize small employers to "play". Keep in mind that larger competitors will likely already be offering health insurance, so offering coverage to employees can increase your competitiveness in attracting talent, especially if you qualify for the tax credit.

If you currently provide insurance to your employees you may be enticed to continue offering the insurance if you receive a tax credit to help offset the costs. Other small employers will want to weigh the options and determine whether providing health coverage is worth the extra cost. In doing so, employers should take the tax credit into account to see if it offsets the costs of insurance enough. Ultimately, it will likely be your budget which determines whether you offer healthcare coverage.

14   *Internal Revenue Service. (2010, May 17). Tax credit for employee health insurance expenses of small employers . Retrieved from http://www.irs.gov/pub/irs-drop/n-10-44.pdf*
15   *Internal Revenue Service. (2010, May 17). Tax credit for employee health insurance expenses of small employers . Retrieved from http://www.irs.gov/pub/irs-drop/n-10-44.pdf*
16   *Internal Revenue Service. (2012, September 26). Small business health-care tax credit for small employers. Retrieved from http://www.irs.gov/uac/Small-Business-Health-Care-Tax-Credit-for-Small-Employers*

SMALL BUSINESS PCORI FEE

Some employers may offer Health Reimbursement Accounts (HRAs) and reimburse their employees for costs not covered by employer-sponsored healthcare coverage, such as out-of-pocket costs or prescription drug costs. Employers that offer HRAs and full insurance are required to pay a $1 fee (it will increase to $2 in 2014) for each participant.[17] This fee will fund the Patient Centered Outcomes Research Institute (PCORI), which performs clinical research on evidence-based medicine, and will be phased out in 2019. The fee will be reported on the IRS Form 720 and must be paid by July 31st of every year. [18]

---

17   *United Healthcare Services, INC. (2012, January 23). Patient-Centered Outcomes Research Institute fee. Retrieved from http://www.uhc.com/united_for_reform_resource_center/health_reform_provisions/patient_centered_outcomes_research_institute_fee.htm*

18   *Internal Revenue Service. (2013, June 07). Patient-Centered Outcomes Research Trust fund fee (IRC 4375, 4376 and 4377): Questions and answers. Retrieved from http://www.irs.gov/uac/Patient-Centered-Outcomes-Research-Trust-Fund-Fee:-Questions-and-Answers*

CHAPTER REVIEW

- Obamacare requires all individuals to have minimum essential coverage.

- Individuals between 100% and 400% of the federal poverty line may be eligible for a premium tax credit to help pay for insurance purchased through an exchange.

- An individual without insurance will be taxed $95 per adult and $47.50 per child (up to $285 per family) or 1.0% of family income, whichever is greater, for not having insurance in 2014.

- An individual without insurance will be taxed $325 per adult and $162.50 per child (up to $975 per family) or 2.0% of family income, whichever is greater, for not having insurance in 2015.

- An individual without insurance will be taxed $695 per adult and $347.50 per child (up to $2,085 per family) or 3.0% of family income, whichever is greater, for not having insurance in 2016.

- Some individuals are exempt from the individual shared responsibility mandate.

- Small employers will be eligible for a tax credit if they have less than 25 FTEs who receive an average annual wage of less than $50,000, and the employer pays at least 50% of healthcare premiums.

- Employers that offer HRAs may have to pay a $1 Patient Centered Outcomes Research Institute fee for each participant.

PART 3:
INSURANCE

9

INSURANCE UNDER OBAMACARE

PURCHASING HEALTHCARE COVERAGE

Insurance companies are required to offer open enrollment periods for small group plans every year from November 15 to December 15. During these open enrollment periods, insurance companies can't impose minimum contribution rules or participation rules. If you are purchasing in the small group market between November 15 and December 15, you don't need to worry about whether you have enough employees participating, or whether you are meeting a minimum dollar contribution. However, if you are purchasing small group insurance during a time other than the November 15 – December 15 open enrollment, the insurance company is allowed to put restrictions on who can or can't enroll in a small group plan, based on minimum contribution or participation. Also, no regulation states an insurance plan must be renewed despite failure to meet minimum contribution and participation rules. This means that although you may be able to purchase healthcare coverage for your employees without meeting the minimum contribution and participation rules, renewing coverage might not be as easy.

This chapter discusses the purchasing of small group plans, not the addition of individuals to a small group plan; refer to Ch. 8 for information about adding individuals to an existing plan.

QUALIFIED HEALTH PLANS

In short, a qualified health plan (QHP) is a plan with an exchange's stamp of approval. QHPs must meet the Obamacare minimum requirements for coverage. The exchanges:

1. Determine the specifications which these plans and insurers must meet
2. Dictate that their rates must be the same on and off the exchange
3. Require at least a Bronze and Silver plan to be offered.

The push toward buying insurance through an exchange most likely results from the fact that exchanges cannot carry any healthcare plans that are not a QHP. In contrast, there is no guarantee that plans offered off the exchange on the private market are QHPs.

INDIVIDUAL EXCHANGES

An exchange provides individuals an online place to shop for insurance and compare plans. It is not the only place to buy insurance. Individuals will still be able to buy healthcare coverage through the private market. However, the exchange is the only place where individuals can apply for a premium tax credit.

Obamacare intended to promote state-created individual exchanges. However, if a state does not create an exchange or partner with the government to do so, then a federally facilitated exchange will be created.[1] This means that instead of the exchange being created and run by the state, it will be created and run by the federal government. The Henry J. Kaiser Family Foundation website lists the states that will have a federally facilitated exchange. If your state is establishing its own exchange, keep in mind that your state's rules may be different from those states with federal exchanges.

EXCHANGES

Federally-Facilitated	State-Facilitated	Jointly-Facilitated
Alabama	California	Arkansas
Alaska	Colorado	Delaware
Arizona	Connecticut	Illinois
Florida	D.C.	Iowa
Georgia	Hawaii	Michigan
Indiana	Idaho	New Hampshire
Kansas	Kentucky	West Virginia
Louisiana	Maryland	
Maine	Massachusetts	
Texas	Minnesota	
Utah	Nevada	
Virginia	New Mexico	
Wisconsin	New York	
Wyoming	Oregon	
Mississippi	Rhode Island	
Missouri	Vermont	
Montana	Washington	
Nebraska		
New Jersey		
North Carolina		
North Dakota		
Ohio		
Oklahoma		
Pennsylvania		
South Carolina		
South Dakota		
Tennessee		

1   The Henry J. Kaiser Family Foundation. (2013, May 2). Establishing health insurance marketplaces: An overview of state efforts. Retrieved from http://kff.org/health-reform/issue-brief/establishing-health-insurance-Exchanges-an-over-view-of/

The exchanges will have open enrollment periods and individuals can only apply for insurance during those time frames unless they experience a qualifying event (discussed below). The open enrollment period for individuals in 2013 will be longer than the standard enrollment period. It will last from October 1, 2013 – March 31, 2014.[2] After 2013, the open enrollment period will always be from October 15 through December 7.[3] If an individual misses the open enrollment period and does not receive insurance from the private market, then that individual will be taxed for not having insurance.

Qualifying events are exceptions which allow individuals to apply for insurance through either the state or federal exchange outside of the open enrollment period, but these individuals will still have a specified period of time in which to enroll. These events include:

- Loss of minimum essential coverage
- Loss of Medicaid
- Change of dependent status
- Relocation to an area where previous insurance is not provided
- An employee's employment ends and the new employer does not offer coverage
- Loss of insurance for valid reason (to be determined by the Department of Health and Human Services)
- Other reasons: please consult the Department of Health

2   *Federal Register. (2012, March 27). Patient Protection and Affordable Care Act; Establishment of exchanges and qualified health plans; Exchange
standards for employers. Retrieved from https://www.federalregister.gov/ar-
ticles/2012/03/27/2012-6125/patient-protection-and-affordable-care-act-establish-
ment-of-exchanges-and-qualified-health-plans*
3   *Federal Register. (2012, March 27). Patient Protection and Affordable Care Act; Establishment of exchanges and qualified health plans; Exchange
standards for employers. Retrieved from https://www.federalregister.gov/ar-
ticles/2012/03/27/2012-6125/patient-protection-and-affordable-care-act-establish-
ment-of-exchanges-and-qualified-health-plans*

and Human Services regulations

It is recommended that you use an insurance broker or navigator to help you buy insurance through an exchange. Some insurance companies may not offer their full insurance portfolio on the exchange or may opt out of offering insurance on the exchange. Other insurance companies may offer all of their plans on the exchange and not use the private market. An insurance broker or navigator can make sure you are aware of all the options available so that you can find insurance that fits you and your employee(s).

BUSINESS EXCHANGES

Businesses with up to 100 FT+FTEs will be able to buy insurance through an exchange separate from the individual exchanges. A small business exchange is called a Small Business Health Options Program (SHOP).[4] Similar to individual exchanges, the SHOP is intended to give employers a place to easily shop for and compare health insurance plans and be certain that the insurance they are buying meets the minimum value mandate laid out by Obamacare. The opening of SHOPs is tiered, depending on the size of your business. exchanges for larger businesses are expected to be established some time in the future.

2014: Employers with up to 50 FT/FTEs can purchase insurance in the SHOPs.[5]

2016: Employers with up to 100 FT/FTEs can purchase insurance in the SHOPs.[6]

---

4   *HealthCare.gov. (2013, June 21). What is the SHOP marketplace? Retrieved from https://www.healthcare.gov/what-is-the-shop-marketplace*
5   *HealthCare.gov. (2013, June 21). What is the SHOP marketplace? Retrieved from https://www.healthcare.gov/what-is-the-shop-marketplace*
6   *HealthCare.gov. (2013, June 21). What is the SHOP marketplace? Retrieved from https://www.healthcare.gov/what-is-the-shop-marketplace*

Note:

In Hawaii, employers with up to 100 FT/FTEs can use the Hawaii SHOP starting in 2014. In other states, 100 FT/FTES have to wait until 2016.

This is important because large employers (50 FT + FTE) are required to provide affordable coverage with minimum value beginning in January 2014, but they will need to purchase it through the private market until these SHOPs are established. This means that large employers will need to scrutinize the insurance they purchase, because plans in the private market are not guaranteed to meet Obamacare standards. So, if you are a large employer, you need to meet these regulations, but there is no guarantee that there will be any plans available that will safeguard you from being penalized by the IRS. If you are a large employer and you don't already have a trusted insurance agent, find one!

Exchanges for employers with more than 100 employees may be developed later.

Employers with less than 25 employees may be able to receive a small employer tax credit by purchasing insurance through a SHOP.[7] However, for employers with 25 to 49 employees, who are too large to receive a tax credit for offering coverage, but too small to receive penalties for not offering coverage, there may be no financial incentive to provide insurance for employees or to purchase insurance through an exchange. If

---

[7]   HealthCare.gov. (2013, June 21). What is the SHOP marketplace? Retrieved from https://www.healthcare.gov/what-is-the-shop-marketplace

an employer with 25-49 employees cancels their insurance plan, employees and their families could to receive a premium tax credit through an individual exchange.

REGULATIONS

Obamacare has brought about a number of changes for insurance companies, including defining some regulations that insurance companies will and will not be allowed to do. For example, insurance companies will not be allowed to:

- Charge up to 50% more for smokers[8]
- Enforce extreme waiting periods[9]
- Reject customers based on pre-existing conditions[10]
- Not guarantee availability and renewability[11]
- Use multiple risk pools[12]

Insurance companies are also not allowed to charge their oldest customers (those over 60 years old) more than three times the rates for their youngest customers (those around 20 years old). This will likely cause the rates for the youngest customers to increase. The Catastrophic Coverage plan has been created for those under 30. These plans have a very high deductible and cover less than 60% of healthcare costs, but are less expensive for healthy people than the metallic

---

8   Kennedy, B. (2013, January 28). Will Obamacare force more smokers to quit? Retrieved from http://money.msn.com/now/post.aspx?post=4d0c1bda-98c3-4c2f-ab2b-d66160f6fe4d
9   Internal Revenue Service. (2010, July 19). Interim final rules for group health plans and health insurance coverage relating to status as a grandfathered health plan under the Patient Protection and Affordable Care Act . Retrieved from http://www.irs.gov/irb/2010-29_IRB/ar08.html
10   HealthCare.gov. (n.d.). How does the healthcare law protect me? Retrieved from https://www.healthcare.gov/how-does-the-health-care-law-protect-me/
11   United Healthcare Services, INC. (n.d.). Dependent (adult child) coverage. Retrieved from http://www.uhc.com/united_for_reform_resource_center/health_reform_provisions/dependent_(adult_child)_coverage.htm
12   United Healthcare Services, INC. (n.d.). Dependent (adult child) coverage. Retrieved from http://www.uhc.com/united_for_reform_resource_center/health_reform_provisions/dependent_(adult_child)_coverage.htm

levels of insurance.

Please consult your insurance broker for a full list of the new regulations for insurance.

LIMITS

Traditionally, many insurance plans have had lifetime and annual limits on the number of specific types of claims the insured can file. Lifetime and annual limits for small groups and individuals are controlled under Obamacare. For a plan that is offered to employees to meet minimum standards under Obamacare, the plan cannot include lifetime limits on any essential health benefits. However, the insurance plan can put lifetime limits on benefits other than the essential health benefits.

Obamacare restricts annual limits for plans before 2014, but prohibits annual limits after 2014 (again, only for small group and individual plans). Plans established with annual limits before 2014 are allowed to have a $2 million annual limit. Plans established after 2014 cannot have lifetime or annual limits.

DEPENDENTS AND ADULT CHILDREN

If you decide to play, the insurance coverage you offer your employees must also be offered to all of their dependents aged 26 or younger. However, you are not required to provide insurance to your employees' spouses. Grandfathered plans are not required to offer coverage to dependents if those dependents are able to get healthcare from another employer.

There has been debate about the exact definition of

"dependent". The IRS needs to issue further guidance to determine exactly to which dependents employers must offer insurance. There is transitional relief in 2014 that allows employers taking steps towards including dependents in coverage to not receive a penalty for not offering coverage.

THE TEN STATUTORY ESSENTIAL HEALTH BENEFITS

Because the primary goal of Obamacare is to offer all Americans quality healthcare, insurance plans for individuals and small groups must offer coverage for 10 categories of essential health benefits.[13] It is important to note that large group plans, self-insured plans, and grandfathered plans are excluded from this requirement.[14] Some states may not require insurance companies/plans to offer all of the required areas of coverage.[15] But, in these cases, states are required to replace that category with another area of coverage. The states will create benchmarks that specify which areas of coverage health plans must include and what the minimum requirements of each category are. If you are self-insured or part of a large group plan, you are not required to have insurance that covers all ten statutory essential health benefits.[16] The essential health benefits are listed on the next page.

13   The Center for Consumer Information & Insurance Oversight. (2013, February 20). Essential Health Benefits standards: Ensuring quality, affordable coverage . Retrieved from http://www.healthcare.gov/news/factsheets/2012/11/ehb11202012a.html
14   United Healthcare Services, INC. (n.d.). Essential Health Benefits . Retrieved from http://www.uhc.com/united_for_reform_resource_center/health_reform_provisions/essential_health_benefits.htm
15   The Center for Consumer Information & Insurance Oversight. (2013, February 20). Essential Health Benefits standards: Ensuring quality, affordable coverage . Retrieved from http://www.healthcare.gov/news/factsheets/2012/11/ehb11202012a.html
16   Internal Revenue Service. (2012, April 30). Notice 2012-31. Retrieved from www.irs.gov/pub/irs-drop/n-12-31.pdf

★ Ten Statutory Essential Benefits

Ambulatory Patient Services	Pediatric Services
Emergency Services	Prescription Drugs
Hospitalization	Laboratory Services
Mental Health and Substance Disorder Services	Rehabilitative and Habilitative Services
Maternity and Newborn Care	Preventive and Wellness and Chronic Disease

FAIR INSURANCE PREMIUMS

Fair insurance premiums prevent insurance companies from varying the price of their premiums for small groups (1-100 individuals in this case) based on health conditions.[17] In the past, insurance companies would estimate the claims that an individual would make and base premiums on that. They are no longer allowed to do that. Instead, there are only a handful of items upon which insurance companies can vary premiums:[18]

- Age
- Family size

---

17   *United Healthcare Services, INC. (2012, August 10). Excise tax on high-cost coverage (Cadillac tax). Retrieved from http://www.uhc.com/united_for_reform_resource_center/health_reform_provisions/excise_tax_on_high_cost_coverage.htm*
18   *United Healthcare Services, INC. (2012, August 10). Excise tax on high-cost coverage (Cadillac tax). Retrieved from http://www.uhc.com/united_for_reform_resource_center/health_reform_provisions/excise_tax_on_high_cost_coverage.htm*

- Tobacco use
- Geography

MEDICAL LOSS RATIO

The Medical Loss Ratio (MLR) indicates the percentage of premiums that an insurance company is using to pay for healthcare costs versus administrative costs.[19] Employers with 50 or more employees cannot have an MLR above 85%. That means 85% of the money paid to insurance companies from premiums has to be used for paying medical expenses. The other 15% can be used for marketing expenses, salaries, or other administrative costs. Similarly, small groups cannot have an MLR above 80%.

If an insurance company is not able to meet the MLR and spends more money from than it should on administrative costs, then the insurance company owes the policyholder a rebate of the money not used for medical coverage.[20]

THE CADILLAC TAX

The Cadillac Tax will apply to employers with high-income employees ($96,900 or more). If your employees are offered health coverage that meets the minimum coverage required by Obamacare, but doesn't exceed 9.5% of their income according to their W-2, you may still be subject to a tax for not offering affordable coverage. Affordable means that the coverage doesn't exceed 9.5% of their income and it doesn't cost more than a set insurance cost threshold. The Cadillac Tax is a 40% excise tax on health insurance plans that cost

19   *U.S. Department of Health & Human Services. (2010, June 30). Medical Loss Ratio (MLR). Retrieved from www.healthcare.gov/glossary/M/medicallossratio. html*
20   *Internal Revenue Service. (2013, June 20). Affordable Care Act tax provisions. Retrieved from http://www.irs.gov/uac/Affordable-Care-Act-Tax-Provisions*

more than $10,200 for an individual or $27,500 for a family.[21] This tax is set to start in 2018.[22] The insurer must pay the excise tax for fully insured plans and the plan administrator must pay the tax for self-funded plans. It is expected that the IRS will release additional information about the Cadillac Tax and the possible threshold adjustments at a later date.

SELF INSURANCE

Self-insured groups don't have to comply with several Obamacare regulations because they are providing insurance without going through an insurance agency. For example, self-insured groups do not have to comply with MLR rules, provide fair insurance premiums, or offer essential health benefits.[23] Remember, insurance companies cannot have some of these limitations. The primary reason businesses might want to look into self-insured group plans is to spread the risks out among a group and to lower the cost of premiums. Please check with a lawyer or insurance professional to determine exactly from which regulations self-insurance is exempt.

Self-insured sponsors are required to pay a tax to fund the Transitional Reinsurance Program (TRP).[24] These taxes will go toward helping insurance companies cover high-cost individuals.[25]

---

21   *United Healthcare Services, INC. (2012, August 10). Excise tax on high-cost coverage (Cadillac tax). Retrieved from http://www.uhc.com/united_for_reform_resource_center/health_reform_provisions/excise_tax_on_high_cost_coverage.htm*
22   *United Healthcare Services, INC. (2012, August 10). Excise tax on high-cost coverage (Cadillac tax). Retrieved from http://www.uhc.com/united_for_reform_resource_center/health_reform_provisions/excise_tax_on_high_cost_coverage.htm*
23   *Commercial Insurance. (2012, July). Self-insured plans under healthcare reform. Retrieved from http://www.ciswv.com/CIS/media/CISMedia/Documents/Self-Insured-Plans-Under-Health-Care-Reform-070312_1.pdf*
24   *Internal Revenue Service. (2012, November 30). ACA Section 1341 Transitional Reinsurance Program FAQs. Retrieved from http://www.irs.gov/uac/Newsroom/ACA-Section-1341-Transitional-Reinsurance-Program-FAQs*
25   *Internal Revenue Service. (2013, July 15). Affordable Care Act tax provisions. Retrieved from http://www.irs.gov/uac/Affordable-Care-Act-Tax-Provisions*

GRANDFATHERED PLANS

A grandfathered plan is any healthcare plan that existed before March 23, 2010 and continuously covered at least one person.[26] You need to check with your insurance agent and keep abreast of HHS notices to find out whether your plan is grandfathered and whether it will remain that way.

These plans may be exempt from some of the requirements of Obamacare, which could encourage employers to keep their grandfathered plans instead of buying new insurance for their employees.[27] Make sure that you check with your insurance agent and keep an eye on HHS notices to see exactly which consumer protections grandfathered plans are exempt from. Some of the Obamacare consumer protections that apply to these plans include:[28]

- Eliminating pre-existing condition exclusions
- Eliminating extreme wait periods
- Banning lifetime and annual limits
- Not rescinding coverage
- Offering coverage to all dependents up to age 26 (for plan years beginning in 2014 and years after)
- Creating transparent coverage explanations and providing coverage definitions
- Reducing healthcare costs

26   *U.S. Department of Health & Human Services. (2010, December 1). Grandfathered health plans. Retrieved from http://www.healthcare.gov/law/features/rights/grandfathered-plans/*
27   *U.S. Department of Health & Human Services. (2010, December 1). Grandfathered health plans. Retrieved from http://www.healthcare.gov/law/features/rights/grandfathered-plans/*
28   *Internal Revenue Service. (2010, July 19). Interim final rules for group health plans and health insurance coverage relating to status as a grandfathered health plan under the Patient Protection and Affordable Care Act . Retrieved from http://www.irs.gov/irb/2010-29_IRB/ar08.html*

Some confusion surrounds grandfathered plans because it is unclear whether they must comply with certain Obamacare regulations from which they are not explicitly exempt. For example, individual plans are not allowed to have unreasonable annual caps under Obamacare, but many grandfathered plans do. Similarly, Obamacare requires emergency care to be treated as in-network, but some grandfathered plans only offer a discount rate on in-network emergency care. It is uncertain how these plans will be treated and whether they will have to comply with Obamacare on these aspects of their plans.

Employers also need to be aware that making changes to grandfathered plans can affect the grandfathered status. For example, the grandfathered status will be lost if a yearly limit is added or made more strict.[29] It is best to consult with your insurance agent and an attorney before making any changes, to ensure that your grandfathered status will not be at risk.

Experts do not know whether grandfathered plans will maintain their status for 2014. The definition of grandfathered plans is expected to change in 2014, but it's unclear the definition will evolve. Healthcare plans won't be able to discriminate by age or health status. It has been proposed that healthcare plans must have a deductible below $2,000 for individual coverage.[30] However, experts don't know how this will apply to grandfathered plans. Some experts believe that the plan will still be compliant with a deductible over $2,500 if the plan is still in the Bronze level. Despite the confusion about the specifics, grandfathered plans will be expected to comply with more regulations in 2014. Since this is constantly changing, you should check with your insurance carrier to

---

29   HealthCare.gov. (n.d.). What if i have a grandfathered health insurance plan? Retrieved from https://www.healthcare.gov/what-if-i-have-a-grandfathered-health-plan
30   Department of Health and Human Services. (2013, February 25). Federal register. Retrieved from http://www.gpo.gov/fdsys/pkg/FR-2013-02-25/pdf/2013-04084.pdf

determine which regulations of Obamacare grandfathered plans are required to follow and which regulations they are exempt from.

Keep in mind that you still need to provide the federally required Employee Disclosures to your staff, even if you have a grandfathered plan. For more information on employee disclosures and notifications, refer to Chapter 6.

INSURANCE TRENDS TO HELP WITH "PAY OR PLAY"

Insurance companies will be taking measures to help employers comply with the "Pay or Play" parts of Obamacare. Some insurance industry experts believe that insurance companies will start offering multiple options for one plan. For example, one plan will be affordable and at the Bronze level. Then, there will be other plan options with higher costs and different coverage options that can be offered to management level employees. This way, you can offer plans that are affordable to many employees, but still offer more benefits to those employees who can afford the higher premiums. It is important that these plans are evaluated by an expert to make sure discrimination laws are not being violated.

Note:

A Bronze level plan means 60% of medical expenses are covered and the insured pays 40% out of pocket. Refer to Chapter 10 for further details about the metallic levels of insurance.

Insurance companies will also relax their participation rules. In the past, a certain percentage of employees were required to enroll in a health coverage plan in order for the employer to offer that plan. Now, insurance companies appear to be reducing or completely eliminating participation rules to satisfy the affordability and minimum value requirements of Obamacare.

CHAPTER REVIEW

- Individuals and small business will be able to purchase insurance through exchanges and the private market.

- Individual exchanges will have open enrollment periods every year for individuals to enroll.

- The Small Business Health Options Program (SHOP) will allow small businesses to shop for insurance.

- Insurance companies will have to follow new regulations when offering insurance, such as not enforcing a waiting period or placing limits on essential health benefits.

- Essential health benefits must be included in individual and small business plans.

- Adjusted Community Ratings prevent insurance companies from varying prices for small groups based on health conditions.

- Self-insured plans do not have to comply with certain Obamacare regulations.

- Grandfathered plans do not have to comply with certain Obamacare regulations.

- Insurance companies will probably start offering multiple options for one plan.

10

WHY METALLIC VALUES ARE BEING IMPLEMENTED

In 2014, insurance companies will begin using standardized tiers of health coverage to name and label their health insurance plans for both businesses and consumers. By using a more universal nomenclature, Obamacare strives to help consumers easily compare plans and be better informed about the differences in the insurance options. At the same time, you will be able to use the names to more easily compare and contrast plans in order to quickly and easily decide which plans to purchase for your employees or business.

Prior to Obamacare, insurance plans were named with a confusing array of letters and numbers, leading to confusion among consumers and businesses. The new terms should make the plans simpler to understand for employees and employers alike. It's meant to be an "apples-to-apples" comparison. In theory, insurance buyers won't have to dig for information anymore. The information will be readily available in the plan's name.

When comparing plans, the actuarial value names (which

communicate the percentage of coverage a buyer is responsible for paying) are an attempt to allow consumers and businesses alike to easily see what coverage is offered and what the cost-sharing requirements are for each plan. These plans are also referred to as "metallic values" because of the names of each tier: Bronze, Silver, Gold, and Platinum. The name values of plans should make it easier to tell which plans offer coverage that fits your budget.

These metallic values will help standardize the value of insurance coverage offered within an insurance plan. By definition, each insurance tier must cover the minimum value requirements (Ch. 9) defined by Obamacare.[1] The minimum value requirement will ensure that any insurance plan purchased by a business does, in fact, meet the requirements of Obamacare – thereby reducing the likelihood of possible fines, penalties, or taxes for providing inadequate healthcare. Although each insurance tier must provide minimum value coverage, the cost-sharing requirements differ by plan (discussed below).

In order to avoid penalties, any employer with more than 100 employees must provide large group health insurance to their FT employees that meets or exceeds the actuarial standards (Bronze, Silver, Gold, or Platinum). However, for now, they'll need to offer insurance without the help of the state or federal exchanges. This is because federal and state exchanges will not be open to these "large employers" until 2017.[2] During the three year gap between 2014 and 2017, these employers will be required to meet the minimum value and the affordability requirements (Ch. 9) established

1   The Center for Consumer Information & Insurance Oversight. (2013, February 20). Essential Health Benefits standards: Ensuring quality, affordable coverage. Retrieved from http://cciio.cms.gov/resources/factsheets/ehb-2-20-2013.html
2   United Healthcare Services, INC. (2013, February 23). Timeline of provisions. Retrieved from http://www.uhc.com/united_for_reform_resource_center/health_reform_provisions.htm

by Obamacare without the help of an exchange. The responsibility for meeting the minimum requirements falls to the employer. As mandated by the law, all employers with less than 100 employees will be able to purchase insurance through small business exchanges in 2014.

THE TIERS OF METALLIC VALUES AND ACTUARIAL VALUES

There are the 5 tiers of actuarial values of insurance:[3]

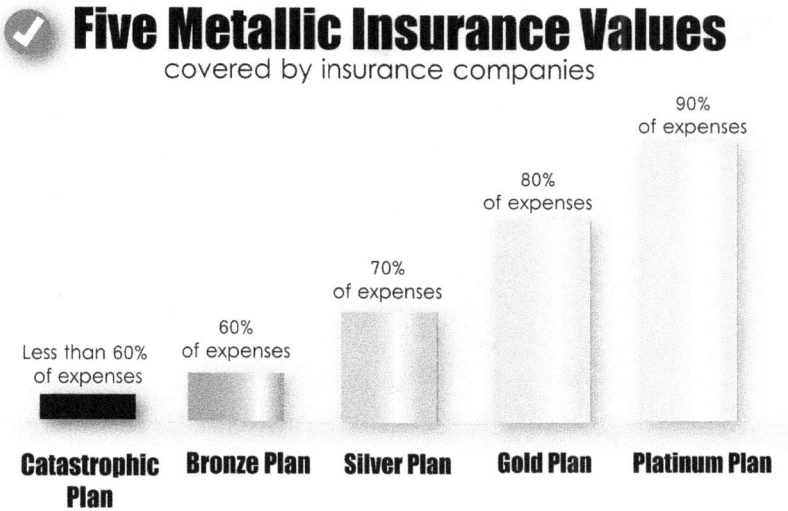

Five Metallic Insurance Values
covered by insurance companies

90% of expenses

80% of expenses

70% of expenses

60% of expenses

Less than 60% of expenses

Catastrophic Plan **Bronze Plan** **Silver Plan** **Gold Plan** **Platinum Plan**

Each Exchange must offer at least a Silver and a Gold plan. The different tiers of insurance are determined by actuarial values. These actuarial values are found based on the average population of the plan. The plan's actuarial value represents

---

3   *Department of Health and Human Services. (2013, February 25). Patient Protection and Affordable Care Act; Standards related to Essential Health Benefits, actuarial value, and accreditation; Final rule. Retrieved from http://www.gpo.gov/ fdsys/pkg/FR-2013-02-25/pdf/2013-04084.pdf*

the percentage of costs the plan would cover for the average population.[4] So, for example, a plan has an actuarial value of 70%, for the standard population, if the plan will cover 70% of healthcare expenses. The law mandates that each plan must be within 2% of its intended actuarial value.[5]

Because the actuarial values are expressed through averages, an individual's out of pocket costs may vary compared to other individuals covered under the same metallic level of insurance, especially if the individuals have different medical needs. Some people may be above the average, and others may be below.

Note:

Catastrophic plans are only for those who are under the age of 30 and are exempt from individual shared responsibility because they cannot find affordable health insurance.

This does not mean that with a Bronze level plan, an employee pays 40% of the healthcare costs. It means that the average employee who has the plan should expect to pay 40% of the healthcare costs. In reality, it may vary as this average is only a guideline.

Different plans within the same level can have different cost-sharing requirements.[6] As long as the correct amount of costs are covered by the insurance company for the metallic level

---

4   The Henry J. Kaiser Family Foundation. (2011, April 17). What the actu-arial values in the Affordable Care Act mean. Retrieved from http://kaiserfamily-foundation.files.wordpress.com/2013/01/8177.pdf
5   The Center for Consumer Information & Insurance Oversight. (2013, Feb-ruary 20). Essential Health Benefits standards: Ensuring quality, affordable cover-age. Retrieved from http://cciio.cms.gov/resources/factsheets/ehb-2-20-2013.html
6   The Henry J. Kaiser Family Foundation. (2011, April 17). What the actu-arial values in the Affordable Care Act mean. Retrieved from http://kaiserfamily-foundation.files.wordpress.com/2013/01/8177.pdf

of a plan, the insurance company can create different ways to split up the costs paid by the consumer. Therefore, co-pays and premiums could vary greatly between plans. For example, a plan may have a $2,000 deductible and 50/50 cost-sharing. Just because the cost-sharing is split 50/50 does not mean that a health insurance plan is below the Bronze level of insurance. All the cost-sharing requirements are taken into account when deciding whether a plan falls under a certain tier of metallic value.

The IRS has suggested basing actuarial value calculations for these plans on four core categories: hospital and emergency room services, physician and mid-level practitioner care, laboratory and imaging services, and pharmacy benefits.[7] If this proposition were to pass, insurance companies would have to make sure that they are covering the actuarial value of costs in each of those categories.

Employees and small businesses will be affected by this because they will be the ones going to the federal and state exchanges to purchase insurance (remember, employers with more than 100 employees cannot shop at exchanges until 2017). Determining which level of coverage to purchase really depends on what fits a business or individual's needs. Since all the levels meet the minimum value requirements that have been set out by Obamacare, businesses can purchase a plan in any level of insurance and be assured that they will not be penalized for not offering minimum value coverage.

---

7   *Internal Revenue Service. (2012, July 30). Minimum value of an employer-sponsored health plan. Retrieved from http://www.irs.gov/pub/irs-drop/n-12-31.pdf*

CHAPTER REVIEW

- Metallic values identify insurance plans' costs to the insured so that they are easier to compare.

- Actuarial values represent the percent of healthcare costs covered by the plan for the average population.

- Metallic values are based on actuarial values: Bronze – 60%, Silver – 70%, Gold – 80%, Platinum – 90%.

PART 4
ACTION PLAN

11

NOW WHAT?

Every executive and business owner is likely asking themselves the proverbial question ... now what? Well, we've got a game plan for you to follow.

DETERMINE WHETHER YOU ARE CONSIDERED A LARGE EMPLOYER

Before making any decisions, you must first determine whether you are considered a large or small employer. The number of employees you employed during the previous calendar year determines large employer status.

You should begin preparing for the large employer calculations sooner rather than later, because the large employer calculation period for 2015 begins January 1, 2014. If you want to make any changes to your employee levels, you should start doing so now.

To determine whether you are a large employer, there are a few steps (listed below). You need to figure out how many people are FT, how to convert your PTs into FTEs, and then we'll find an average employment level for the year.

Step 1. Finding the FT

Calculate the number of FT employees you employed. To calculate FT employees in a given month, determine which employees worked 130 hours per month and simply do a head-count. We aren't concerned with weekly hours worked because the IRS has proposed that it will assess penalties based on monthly hours worked. See Chapter 2: Seasonal Employee Exemption to determine whether you need to include seasonal workers.

Step 1:

JULY 2013

Employee	Total hours
Jenny Jones	180
Thomas Scott	190
Liz Phelps	175
Zach Thomas	150
Jessica Phillips	115
Bob Jennings	150
Chris Ryans	150

*All of these employees, except Jessica Phillips, are full-time employees.

Step 2. Finding the FTE

To calculate FTEs for the same month, add up all of the hours worked by part-time employees during the month (not greater than 130 per person), and divide the total by 120. The resulting calculation should be rounded down (or just remove the decimal portion), and this result is the number of FTE employees for the month. FTE is a derived calculation of the number of part-time (PT) employees it takes to work the equivalent number of hours that a FT employee works.

JULY 2013	
Employee	**Total hours**
Jessi Scott	75
Jack Stone	55
Eliza Heigle	75
Tom Thomas	100
Ally Phillips	100
John Pitt	50
Carol Harding	75
Total:	**530**

Monthly total of part-time hours: 530
Monthly FTE: 530/120 = 4

Step 3. Finding the average of FTs and FTEs

Add up your FT totals for each month, then divide the result by 12. Separately, add up your FTE totals for each month and divide that result by 12. You now know how many FTs and FTEs you employed, on average, per month.

Month	# of Full-Time Employees
January	51
February	50
March	50
April	45
May	35
June	35
July	35
August	40
September	40
October	50
November	55
December	60
Total:	546

Monthly Total of FT Employees for the Year: 546
Average of FT Employees: 546/12= 46

Month	# of Full-Time Equivalent Employees
January	4
February	5
March	5
April	15
May	15
June	15
July	10
August	10
September	10
October	15
November	15
December	15
Total:	134

Year total of FTE Employees: 134
Average of FT Employees: 134/12= 11

Step 4. Finding the FT + FTE.

Add your monthly average number of FT employees to your monthly average number of FTE employees. If the result contains a decimal, round down.[1] If this number is 50 or more, you are considered a large employer under Obamacare. If you have an average of 49 or fewer FTs + FTEs, you are not considered a large employer under Obamacare.

$$46.8 + 11.1 = 57.9 = 57$$

You are a large employer!

You can use software, a spreadsheet, or even a chalkboard to calculate your large employer status, but you need to do it now. This will help you decide whether you want to hire more people, cut hours, or increase overtime to help prepare for Obamacare. Speak with your IT team so that you can easily track hours. Be sure your HR team is aware of your decisions to hire more or less people. Prepare yourself now for the implementation of employer shared responsibility and the penalties that come with it in 2015. Remember, your employment levels in 2014 determine your 2015 status.

---

1   Department of the Treasury. (2012, December 27). Shared responsibility for employers regarding health coverage. Retrieved from http://www.irs.gov/pub/newsroom/reg-138006-12.pdf

I'M A SMALL EMPLOYER

As a small employer, you still need to be aware of the law and how it will affect you and your employees. If you are close to the 50 FT + FTE mark, it is extremely important to monitor your staff now. Don't exceed 50 FT + FTE employees if you want to avoid becoming a large employer. Make sure your labor numbers stay consistent and pay attention to hiring practices. Increasing hours of PT employees could increase your FTE, thereby making your FT + FTE calculation larger.

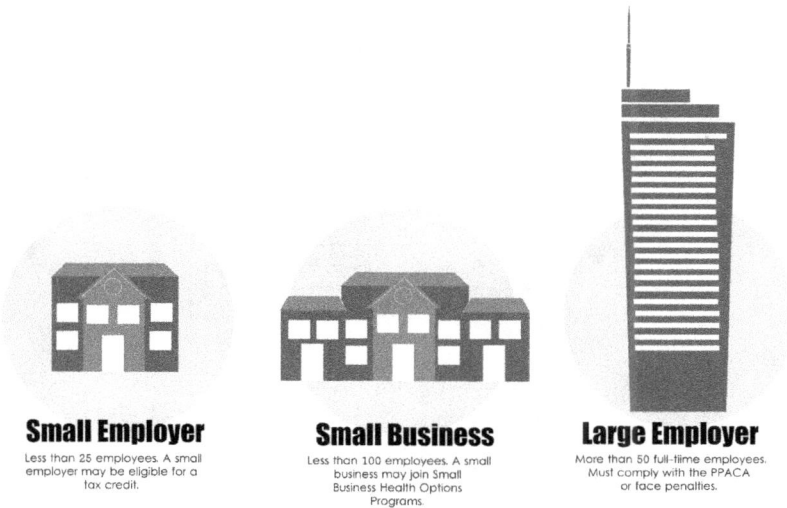

Small Employer
Less than 25 employees. A small employer may be eligible for a tax credit.

Small Business
Less than 100 employees. A small business may join Small Business Health Options Programs.

Large Employer
More than 50 full-time employees. Must comply with the PPACA or face penalties.

If you have fewer than 25 FTE employees, you may be eligible for a small employer tax credit to help pay for healthcare, should you choose to offer it to employees. To calculate your FTEs to determine whether you are eligible for the tax credit, do the following:

Step 1:
Determine how many hours each employee worked for the whole year. Do not exceed 2,080 hours per employee. So, if Jane worked 2,100 hours, reduce it to 2,080.

Step 2:
Find your total labor hours for the year. Add up all FT and PT employee hours worked for the year, excluding owners, family members, and seasonal employees.

	Joe	Sally	Molly	Chris
January	150 hrs	165 hrs	120 hrs	150 hrs
February	150 hrs	165 hrs	120 hrs	150 hrs
March	150 hrs	165 hrs	120 hrs	150 hrs
April	150 hrs	165 hrs	120 hrs	150 hrs
May	150 hrs	165 hrs	120 hrs	150 hrs
June	150 hrs	165 hrs	120 hrs	150 hrs
July	150 hrs	165 hrs	120 hrs	150 hrs
August	150 hrs	165 hrs	120 hrs	150 hrs
September	150 hrs	165 hrs	120 hrs	150 hrs
October	150 hrs	165 hrs	120 hrs	150 hrs
November	150 hrs	165 hrs	120 hrs	150 hrs
December	150 hrs	165 hrs	120 hrs	150 hrs
Total Hours:	**1800**	**1980**	**1440**	**1800**

Total: 7020

Step 3:
Divide the sum from Step 2 by 2,080. If the result contains a decimal, round down. If the result is less than 25, you may be eligible for the tax credit and you should proceed to Step 4. If the total is 25 or more, you are not eligible for the tax credit and you should stop here.

Step 4:
Determine the average salary of your employees. Add up all of their salaries and divide that total by your FT + FTE number. Round that result down to the nearest thousand.

☑ $1800 + 1980 + 1440 + 1800 = 7020$

☑ $7020/2080 = 3 \text{ FTEs}$

You may be eligible for a tax credit

For example, if the result is $25,799, you will round down to $25,000. If the result is less than $50,000, you may be eligible for the tax credit and you should proceed to Step 5. If the total is more than $50,000, you are not eligible for the tax credit and you should stop here. To be eligible:

Average Salary / (FTs + FTEs) < **$50,000**

Step 5:
Determine whether the insurance you offer covers at least 50% of the premiums based on individual health cost rates. If you cover at least 50%, you are eligible for the tax credit. IRS Form 8941 can help you determine the exact amount of

the tax credit you will receive. Please consult your tax advisor to make sure your calculations are correct according to the latest information presented by the IRS.

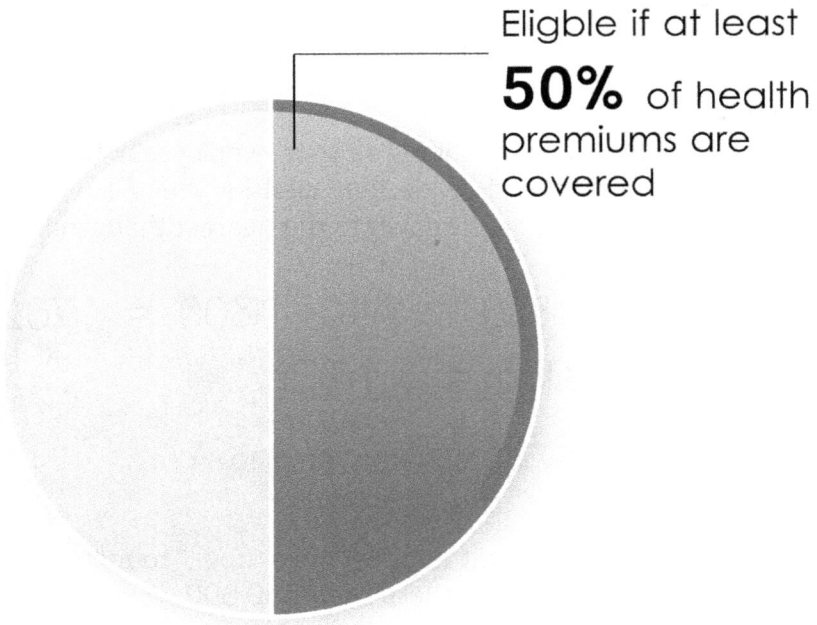

Eligble if at least

50% of health premiums are covered

Even though you are not a large employer, you still may be subject to taxes. If you offer your employees a Health Reimbursement Account (HRA) as well as full insurance, you will have to pay a Patient Centered Outcomes Research Institute (PCORI) fee to help fund clinical research. This fee is $1 for each participant, and will increase to $2 in 2014. Employers will be required to report the fee on IRS Form 720 and pay it by July 31 of each year.

Your employees will want to know how Obamacare will affect them. You, as their employer, may be their first line of reference. By preparing yourself to answer their questions, you will increase employee morale by demonstrating that you care for their well-being and are well-informed about the law.

I'M A LARGE EMPLOYER

As a large employer, you are required to offer affordable and minimum value coverage to all of your FT employees. If you don't, you are liable to receive two penalties: Penalty A and Penalty B.

- **Penalty A:** If you do not offer your FT employees healthcare coverage and one employee receives a premium tax credit from an exchange, then you will be penalized $2,000 x (# of FT - 30). There is a safe harbor in place that protects employers in case of minor errors. The safe harbor prevents you from being penalized if you do not offer coverage to 5% of your FT employees or 5 employees, whichever is greater.

- **Penalty B:** If you do offer your FT employees healthcare coverage, but it is not affordable (if it costs at least 9.5% of an employee's W-2 wage) or it is not of minimum value (if the plan fails to cover at least 60% of medical costs), then you will be penalized $3,000 for each employee who receives a premium tax credit.

Because penalties are based on your number of FT employees, it is very important to determine which employees are FT so that you know which employees to offer coverage to. The two ways to determine FT status are the guess and check method and the IRS lookback measurement method. These methods were covered more comprehensively in Chapters 4 and 5.

You can use the guess and check method to retroactively

determine whether your employees are FT or PT for each month, and offer coverage accordingly. Alternatively, you can proactively guess how many hours your employees will work, and offer coverage based on that estimate. However, this method is risky for two very big reasons: inaccuracy and delay. Many employee's statuses constantly change, so proactively guessing at the number of hours they will work is likely a shot in the dark, with plenty of room for error. Retroactively calculating labor hours takes too long, because you won't know whether you owe someone healthcare coverage until after the fact – which means you could face a penalty for not offering the coverage at the time. However, the guess and check method requires the least number of dedicated Obamacare personnel and is less time-consuming than the IRS lookback measurement method.

The second method was established as a safe harbor by the IRS and is called the lookback measurement method. This method essentially measures an employee as PT or FT and then locks in their status. There are 3 periods associated with the lookback measurement method, one of which is optional. The measurement period must be between 3 and 12 months long. You measure an employee's hours during this period. If the employee works 130 hours a month, the employee is considered FT. The stability period then locks in that employee's status as FT (PT if the employee was measured as working less than 130 hours a month) and lasts as long as the measurement period, or 6 months. Whether an employee's hours increase or decrease, the PT or FT status for that employee remains the same. You also have the option to include an administrative period of 90 days. This period is used for checking an employee's status and enrolling the employee in healthcare coverage. Then, the process starts all over again.

The lookback measurement method provides you with more

security than the guess and check method because you don't have to guess which employees will be FT for a given month. Instead, an employee's FT status is locked in, giving you a specific time range in which you are required to offer health insurance.

All employers, large and small, are required to provide their employees with a notification of exchanges by October 2013. The form you will use for this notification (OMB 1210-0149) has been released by the Department of Labor and can be found on our website: www.EmployersAndObamacare.com.

Finally, one of the most important things you must to do to prepare for the implementation of employer shared responsibility in 2015 is to prepare your employees. Get in touch with your IT team to make sure you have methods in place to track employees' hours and PT or FT status. Make sure your HR team is on board, understands the law, and is prepared to make necessary accommodations. Many of the reporting requirements will involve them. You also need to make sure they are aware of employment decisions you might make to prepare for employer shared responsibility.

12

SCENARIOS AND EXAMPLES

The big decision now falls to you. You need to decide how you want to prepare for the implementation of employer shared responsibility in 2015. If you are a not a large employer, you need to determine whether you are eligible for the small employer tax credit and whether you want to offer health insurance to your employees.

If you are a large employer, you have more questions to ask yourself. Do you want to pay the fine or play by offering healthcare? Do you want to offer skinny plans? Do you want to decrease the number of FT employees and thereby your potential costs for healthcare coverage or penalties? Can you afford to offer more overtime to facilitate this change?

Once you've decided how to proceed, make sure you sit down with your team so that everyone is on the same page. If you want to increase your number of part-time workers, you don't want your HR team to continue hiring full-time workers. That seems like a lot of options, but we lay it out for you and have some examples to help you sort it all out.

Please note, the following scenarios are just examples to give you an idea of how to calculate costs. This is not intended to be legal or tax advice. Please consult your tax advisor when making decisions related to insurance and potential penalties.

THE SMALL EMPLOYER TAX CREDIT OPTION

If you have less than 25 FTE employees and pay your employees an average wage of less than $50,000, you need to decide whether to offer your employees health insurance and receive a tax credit. Remember, you have to pay 50% of the healthcare premiums for your employees in order to be eligible. Keep in mind that employees will be looking for employers who provide healthcare coverage once individual responsibility begins in 2014, especially if they are PT. Therefore, not offering health insurance could increase your labor costs. On the other hand, offering insurance to employees can be costly, especially since you have to pay 50% of their healthcare premiums based on the individual rate to receive the tax credit. It's important to weigh the pros and cons of each option, and consult your tax advisor to determine the exact amount of the credit.

OPTION 1: TO PAY OR PLAY?

The decision to either pay or play relies entirely upon what is best for your company and its unique circumstances. One consideration you will need to make regarding this choice will be your budget, as the penalty fees for not offering health insurance may either be more or less than the cost of offering healthcare coverage. Also, remember that providing these benefits may lead to increased employee morale and decreased turnover.

By not offering insurance, you may see an increase in turnover rates. Employees will be required to have health insurance because of the individual mandate. If they do not receive insurance from their job, they may seek another job that does offer coverage.

OPTION 2: TO OFFER SKINNY PLANS?

Skinny plans provide you with an option to avoid penalty A. By offering your employees a skinny plan, or a plan with minimum coverage (not affordable or of minimum value), you are providing them with coverage with the hope they will not go to an exchange to purchase health insurance. If only a few FT employees get a premium tax credit from the exchange, which will trigger penalty B, the total cost of the penalties will be less than not offering insurance. The reason for this is that penalty B is calculated by the number of FT employees that get a premium tax credit, not all of your FT employees. If you have 60 FT employees, and only 10 FT employees receive a premium tax credit, then you will only have to pay a penalty for those 10 FT employees. More information about penalties can be found in Chapter 3.

OPTION 3: TO INCREASE THE NUMBER OF PT EMPLOYEES?

Since the penalties are based on your number of FT employees, you can reduce their potential costs by reducing your number of FT employees. To achieve this result you need to fire your FT employees or cut their hours. Remember, for healthcare purposes, FT employees work 130 hours a month or an average of 30 hours a week. Keep in mind that it might be harder to attract new workers to your company if you are only hiring PT workers and your turnover rate may increase.

It is also important to remember that the cost of an employee leaving the company and hiring a new one may be expensive. This includes several expenses that add up. After an employee has put in his 2 weeks notice, his productivity will probably go down. Managers will spend time offboarding the employee, and both will have to participate in an exit interview. Then, the company will need to spend time and money marketing the job to find a new employee, printing applications, and performing drug tests. Management will be spending time reviewing applications and conducting interviews. Once a new employee is hired, training will be required. This will lead to inefficiency for both the new employee and the trainer. These factors could compel you to offer coverage to increase employee retention.

OPTION 4: TO OFFER OVERTIME?

You may decide that you want to avoid being a large employer altogether by decreasing your number of employees. This could make you short on labor. You could increase your FT employee's hours and give them overtime thus reducing your head count. You need to determine whether it will be more cost-effective to pay for overtime for fewer employees in order to avoid large employer status, or to pay or play with more employees and becoming a large employer.

EXAMPLE 1

A Ma and Pa store has one location and employs 15 FT employees that each work 40 hours a week. Both Ma and Pa are owners of the store and work full-time. The first thing Ma and Pa need to do is determine whether they are a large employer. Since they have less than 50 employees, they are not, but let's work through the calculations anyway.

Large Employer Calculation:

Determine the number of FT employees for each month.

To calculate the yearly average of full-time employees, add up the monthly totals and divide by 12.

Month	# of Full-Time Employees
January	20
February	15
March	10
April	15
May	18
June	15
July	12
August	10
September	20
October	20
November	10
December	15
Total:	**180**

$$180/12 = \boxed{15}$$

The number is less than 50, so Ma and Pa are not large employers. However, Ma and Pa may be eligible for a small employer tax credit. Now, Ma and Pa need to calculate their number of FTEs using the small employer tax credit's method.

Small Employer Tax Credit Option:

Each employee works 2,080 hours a year. First, add up the number of hours each employee worked for the year, not exceeding 2,080 per employee, excluding the owners:

Employee	Yearly Hours Worked
Jessica	2,080
Thomas	2,080
Chris	2,080
Jennifer	2,080
Mitchell	2,080
Kelly	2,080
Sarah	2,080
Paul	2,080
Tom	2,080
Becky	2,080
Sandra	2,080
Julie	2,080
Joey	2,080
Sam	2,080
April	2,080
Total:	**31,200**

31,200 / 2,080 = 15

# of FTEs for the year

To calculate the yearly hours worked, add up the monthly totals and divide by 2,080. This determines the year's FTE, which in this case is 15.

Next, calculate the employees' average yearly wages (which must be below $50,000):

5 of the employees are paid $12 an hour. Their yearly wages are 2,080 hrs worked x $12 = $24,960. Ten of the employees are paid $10 an hour. Their yearly wages are 2,080 hrs worked x $10 = $20,800. Add up all the employees' wages, excluding the owners, family members, etc (Ch. 8):

Employee	Yearly Hours Worked (Hours worked X Wage)
Jessica	$12 x 2,080 = $24,960
Thomas	$12 x 2,080 = $24,960
Chris	$12 x 2,080 = $24,960
Jennifer	$12 x 2,080 = $24,960
Mitchell	$12 x 2,080 = $24,960
Kelly	$10 x 2,080 = $20,800
Sarah	$10 x 2,080 = $20,800
Paul	$10 x 2,080 = $20,800
Tom	$10 x 2,080 = $20,800
Becky	$10 x 2,080 = $20,800
Sandra	$10 x 2,080 = $20,800
Julie	$10 x 2,080 = $20,800
Joey	$10 x 2,080 = $20,800
Sam	$10 x 2,080 = $20,800
April	$10 x 2,080 = $20,800

= $332,800

Divide the sum by the number of FTEs:

$$\$332{,}800 \; / \; 15 \; = \; \$22{,}186.66$$

Rounding down to the nearest thousand, the average yearly wages are $22,000.

Since the average of the yearly wages is below $50,000, Ma and Pa are eligible for a tax credit if they offer healthcare that is affordable and of minimum value for their employees, and pay at least 50% of the premiums.

Ma and Pa's next step is to calculate the amount of their small employer tax credit. This can be done using IRS Form 8941. However, we will also work through and explain it here.

If they offer insurance to their FT employees, which hypothetically costs $5,000 an employee for single coverage for a year, the total costs would be:

$5,000 x 15 FT = $75,000 a year

Now Ma and Pa need to compare what they paid for insurance to what the average cost for insurance in their state was (IRS Form 8941 Instructions). Let's say Ma and Pa are located in Texas. The average cost of single coverage is $5,222. So, the cost of offering coverage that costs $5,222 to 15 employees is:

$5,222 x 15 = $78,300 a year

The amount that is used for remaining calculations is the

smaller amount, or the amount Ma and Pa paid. Now, Ma and Pa need to multiply the amount they paid by the tax credit percentage which has been determined for the year. We are calculating the tax credit for 2013, so the percentage is 35% or 0.35:

$75,000 x 0.35 = $26,250

If Ma and Pa had less than 10 FTEs, they would receive a tax credit of $26,250. But Ma and Pa employ more than 10 FTEs, so we need to determine what the credit will be reduced by. To do that, determine how many FTEs over 10 Ma and Pa have:

15 FTE - 10 = 5 FTE

Divide that by the total number of FT employees, and round to three places after the decimal.

5/15 = .333

Multiply that result by the 35% of health insurance premiums that Ma and Pa pay:

$26,250 x 0.333 = $8,741.25

Subtract the above amount from the 35% of health insurance premiums that Ma and Pa pay:

$26,250 - $8,741.25 = $17,508.75

This is the small employer tax credit Ma and Pa will receive. Now, let's see how much Ma and Pa will be paying for healthcare for their employees after the tax credit:

$75,000 - $17,508.75 = $57,491.25 a year

CONCLUSION

Ma and Pa need to decide if it is in their budget to offer healthcare coverage to their employees. They also need to consider the costs of increased turnover rates. Their employees will probably look for a job that does offer health benefits because every American will be required to have health insurance in 2014 or receive a tax.

EXAMPLE 2

Bob is a small independent franchise owner. He has two locations of his restaurant, each of which employs 7 FT managers and 36 PT employees who work an average of 60 hours a month. Since Bob is the owner of both locations, the locations are calculated together to determine large employer status.

Large Employer Calculation:
Determine the number of FT employees for each month at each location.

Find the average number of FT employees for the year for each location by adding up the total of FT employees for each month and dividing by 12. Both locations have an average of 7 full-time employees.

Add the yearly averages for each location together: 7 + 7 = 14. This is the total of FT employees that Bob employs.

✔ FT Calculation

Location 1:

Month	# of Full-Time Employees
January	7
February	7
March	7
April	7
May	7
June	7
July	7
August	7
September	7
October	7
November	7
December	7
Total:	**84**

Average # of FT Employees:

84 / 12 = ⑦

Location 2:

Month	# of Full-Time Employees
January	7
February	7
March	7
April	7
May	7
June	7
July	7
August	7
September	7
October	7
November	7
December	7
Total:	**84**

Average # of FT Employees:

84 / 12 = ⑦

7 + 7 = ⭐ 14 **Total # of FTs for Bob**

Next, add up the total number of hours PT employees worked for each month at each location.

✅ FTE Calculation

Location 1:

Month	# of PT Hours Worked	# of FTEs (Hours worked / 120)
January	2,160	2,160 / 120 = 18
February	2,160	2,160 / 120 = 18
March	2,160	2,160 / 120 = 18
April	2,160	2,160 / 120 = 18
May	2,160	2,160 / 120 = 18
June	2,160	2,160 / 120 = 18
July	2,160	2,160 / 120 = 18
August	2,160	2,160 / 120 = 18
September	2,160	2,160 / 120 = 18
October	2,160	2,160 / 120 = 18
November	2,160	2,160 / 120 = 18
December	2,160	2,160 / 120 = 18
Total:		216

Yearly FTE Average: 216 / 12 = 18

Location 2:

Month	# of PT Hours Worked	# of FTEs (Hours worked / 120)
January	2,160	2,160 / 120 = 18
February	2,160	2,160 / 120 = 18
March	2,160	2,160 / 120 = 18
April	2,160	2,160 / 120 = 18
May	2,160	2,160 / 120 = 18
June	2,160	2,160 / 120 = 18
July	2,160	2,160 / 120 = 18
August	2,160	2,160 / 120 = 18
September	2,160	2,160 / 120 = 18
October	2,160	2,160 / 120 = 18
November	2,160	2,160 / 120 = 18
December	2,160	2,160 / 120 = 18
Total:		216

Yearly FTE Average: 216 / 12 = 18

18 + 18 = 36 ⭐ Total # of FTEs for Bob at both locations

Once you've done that, divide the total number of monthly hours worked at each location for each month by 120 to determine each month's FTE:

Add up the FTEs for each month for each location and divide

by 12 to get the yearly FTE average. As you can see, both locations have a yearly FTE average of 18.

Add up the yearly FTE average for each location:

18 + 18 = 36

This is the total number of FTEs that Bob employs.

Add the total number of FT employees and the total number of FTEs:

36 FTEs + 14 FTs = 50

Bob is a large employer!

Since this number is 50 or more, Bob is considered a large employer under Obamacare and must offer healthcare coverage to all FT employees to avoid penalties. Now Bob needs to consider his options.

OPTION 1:

If Bob decides to not offer health insurance to his FT employees and pay the penalty, the maximum amount he will pay, according to Penalty A, is $0:

Penalty A: $2,000 x (# FT - 30)
Penalty A: $2,000 x (14 - 30)
Penalty A: $2,000 x (-16)

Bob does not have enough FT employees to pay Penalty A if an employee receives a premium tax credit from an exchange (which is why there is a negative number). He is not eligible to receive Penalty B because he doesn't offer insurance at all. Therefore, his employees can't receive a premium tax credit because their employer's insurance isn't affordable or of minimum value, which is what Penalty B is based on.

However, not offering insurance could be detrimental. Since his employees are now required to have health insurance because of individual shared responsibility, they may seek another job that does offer health insurance. This could increase his turnover rates. He can choose to play and offer insurance that is affordable and of minimum value. Hypothetically, costs for such insurance would be about $6,000 per year per employee for individual coverage. If Bob offered healthcare that meets the minimum Obamacare requirements to all his FT employees, the cost would be:

$6,000 x 14 FT = $84,000 a year

That's a big expense, especially when compared to the $0 penalty for not offering insurance. But offering affordable and minimum value coverage to FT employees is not the only way to go.

OPTION 2:

Bob can choose to offer a skinny plan, which offers bare bones coverage that doesn't meet the affordability and minimum value requirements. Bob will not receive Penalty A, which leaves Penalty B. Remember, Penalty B is triggered by an employee refusing his insurance and receiving a premium tax credit from an exchange. By offering a skinny plan, Bob is banking on his employees accepting his offered coverage and not going to an exchange. Hypothetically, a skinny plan would cost Bob $1,200 an employee a year. So, the cost for offering a skinny plan to all his FT employees would be:

$1,200 x 14 FT = $16,800 a year

Bob may still receive Penalty B though. Penalty B is based on the number of employees who receive a premium tax credit because their employer's coverage is not affordable or of minimum value. The maximum penalty Bob might incur if all his employees go to an exchange and receive a premium tax credit is:

Penalty B: $3,000 x FT employees that receive premium tax credit
Penalty B: $3,000 x 14 FT employees that receive premium tax credit
Penalty B: $42,000 a year

However, Penalty B cannot exceed the cost of Penalty A, which in this case is $0. If all the FT employees go to an exchange and receive a premium tax credit, then Bob won't have to pay for coverage for anyone. The result would be:

$0 + $0 = $0 a year

Therefore, the most Bob could pay when offering a skinny plan insurance is the actual cost of insurance: $16,800 a year.

OPTION 3:

Bob can also decide whether he wants to increase his number of PT employees, resulting in a reduction of his number of FT employees. He would have to offer coverage to fewer employees, which would reduce the costs of offering coverage to FT employees and could reduce the costs of potential penalties. In this case, reducing the number of FT employees would not affect the cost of penalties because Penalty A and Penalty B for Bob's franchises are $0. However, it could affect the cost of offering regular or skinny health insurance plans to his employees. For example, if Bob reduced the number of FT employees at each location to 5 (for a total of 10 FT employees), the cost of healthcare coverage that meets the requirements of Obamacare is:

$6,000 x 10 FT = $60,000 a year

Bob could also choose to offer the 10 FT employees skinny insurance:

$1,200 x 10 FT = $12,000 a year

To ensure he has the right amount of staff, Bob will need to increase his number of PT employees to 40, which could result in higher turnover rates.

Bob needs to decide what is best for his company: keeping his 14 FT employees or reducing them down to 10 and increasing his turnover rate.

OPTION 4:

Finally, Bob can try to avoid large employer status by offering overtime to his FT employees, and decreasing his number of PT employees. If he reduces his head count so that it is below the 50 FT + FTE, then he is not required to offer healthcare to his FT employees. However, he needs to take into account the additional cost of paying overtime.

First, let's figure out by how many PT employees Bob needs to reduce his labor. Currently, Bob employs 50 FT + FTE employees between both his locations, 14 total FT employees, and 72 PT employees who work 60 hours a month. If Bob reduces his PT employees by 1 (and employs 36 employees at one location and 35 at the other), he should be under the 50 FT + FTE mark, because one PT employee works 60 hours a month, or half of an FTE. That's subtracting .5 from his 50 FT + FTE mark, which leaves Bob with 49.5 FT+ FTEs.

Let's double check by doing the large employer calculation again:

Determine the number of FT employees for each month at each location and find the average number of FT employees for the year for each location by adding up the total FT employees for each month and dividing by 12.

Next, add the yearly averages for each location together to get the total number of FT employees that Bob employs.

FT Calculation

Location 1:

Month	# of Full-Time Employees
January	7
February	7
March	7
April	7
May	7
June	7
July	7
August	7
September	7
October	7
November	7
December	7
Total:	**84**

Average # of FT Employees:

84 / 12 = 7

Location 2:

Month	# of Full-Time Employees
January	7
February	7
March	7
April	7
May	7
June	7
July	7
August	7
September	7
October	7
November	7
December	7
Total:	**84**

Average # of FT Employees:

84 / 12 = 7

7 + 7 = 14   Total # of FTs for Bob

Add up the total number of hours PT employees worked for each month at each location. Divide the total number of monthly hours worked at each location for each month by 120 to determine each month's FTE:

✓ FTE Calculation

Location 1:

Month	# of PT Hours Worked	# of FTEs (Hours worked / 120) *Make sure to round down
January	2,160	2,160 / 120 = 18
February	2,160	2,160 / 120 = 18
March	2,160	2,160 / 120 = 18
April	2,160	2,160 / 120 = 18
May	2,160	2,160 / 120 = 18
June	2,160	2,160 / 120 = 18
July	2,160	2,160 / 120 = 18
August	2,160	2,160 / 120 = 18
September	2,160	2,160 / 120 = 18
October	2,160	2,160 / 120 = 18
November	2,160	2,160 / 120 = 18
December	2,160	2,160 / 120 = 18
Total:		(216)

Yearly FTE Average: 216 / 12 = 18

Location 2:

Month	# of PT Hours Worked	# of FTEs (Hours worked / 120) *Make sure to round down
January	2,100	2,100 / 120 = 17
February	2,100	2,100 / 120 = 17
March	2,100	2,100 / 120 = 17
April	2,100	2,100 / 120 = 17
May	2,100	2,100 / 120 = 17
June	2,100	2,100 / 120 = 17
July	2,100	2,100 / 120 = 17
August	2,100	2,100 / 120 = 17
September	2,100	2,100 / 120 = 17
October	2,100	2,100 / 120 = 17
November	2,100	2,100 / 120 = 17
December	2,100	2,100 / 120 = 17
Total:		(204)

Yearly FTE Average: 204 / 12 = 17

18 + 17 = 35 **Total # of FTEs for Bob**

The FTE calculation for location 1 is the same as before because the number of PT employees did not change there. Add up the FTEs for each month for each location and divide by 12 to get the yearly FTE average: At location 1, we have a yearly FTE average of 18. At location 2, we have a yearly FTE average of 17.

Add up the yearly FTE average for each location:

17 FTEs + 18 FTs = (35)

This is the total number of FTEs that Bob employs.

Add the total number of FT employees and the total number of FTEs:

35 FTEs + 14 FTs = (49)

Since this number is below 50, Bob will not be considered a large employer if he reduces his number of PT employees. However, now he may offer overtime to his FT employees at location 2 to make sure that he has enough staff. This could end up costing Bob some money, so let's do some calculations.

Bob's FT employees are paid $13.00 an hour, and his PT employees are paid $8.00 an hour. The monthly cost of the PT employee (works 60 hours a month) is:

$8.00 x 60 hrs = $480 a month

Those 60 hours a month now need to be given over to his FT staff so that he has enough staff. Since his FT staff already work 40 hours a week, Bob will need to pay them overtime. If he spreads the 60 hours between his 7 FT employees at location 2, then he can pay time and a half for those 60 hours:

$13.00 x 1.5 OT = $19.50 an hour
$19.50 x 60 hrs = $1,170 a month

The difference between paying overtime to Bob's FT employees and not reducing his number of PT employees is:

$1,170 – $480 = $690 more a month.

Over the course of a year, this adds up to:

$690 a month x 12 months = $8,280

CONCLUSION

If Bob can afford to offer overtime to his FT staff to avoid being a large employer, he must keep in mind that his turnover may increase. Employees will be looking for jobs that provide healthcare insurance since they are required to have it starting January 1, 2014 in order to avoid paying an individual fine. Therefore, his employees might continue to look for an individual job that offers healthcare benefits.

EXAMPLE 3

A non-profit organization has 7 locations, each of which employs 50 FT employees and 100 PT employees who work an average of 100 hours a month. For location 1, the number of PT employees varies from month to month. Since one organization controls all 7 locations, the locations are calculated together when determining large employer status.

Large Employer Calculation:

Determine the number of FT employees for each month at each location.

Next, find the average number of FT employees for the year for each location by adding up the total number of FT employees for each month and dividing by 12.

Location 1,2,3,4,5,6,7:

Month	# of Full-Time Employees
January	50
February	50
March	50
April	50
May	50
June	50
July	50
August	50
September	50
October	50
November	50
December	50
Total:	**600**

Average yearly FTs: 600 / 12 = 50

In this example, each location has a yearly FT average of 50.

Add the yearly averages of FT employees for each location together:

50 + 50 + 50 + 50 + 50 + 50 + 50 = 350

This is the total of FT employees that the non-profit organization employs.

Add up the total number of hours all PT employees worked for each month at each location. Then, divide the number of monthly hours worked at each location for each month by 120. The result is the month's FTE.

Once you have done this for every month, add up the FTEs for each month for each location and divide by 12 to get the yearly FTE average.

Location 1:

Month	# of Part-Time Employees	# of FTEs (hours worked / 120) *Make sure to round down
January	10,100	10,100/120=84
February	10,200	10,200/120=85
March	10,200	10,200/120=85
April	10,300	10,300/120=85
May	10,200	10,200/120=85
June	10,200	10,200/120=85
July	10,100	10,100/120=84
August	10,200	10,200/120=85
September	10,100	10,100/120=84
October	10,000	10,000/120=83
November	10,000	10,000/120=83
December	9,900	10,000/120=83
Total:		996

Average yearly FTEs: 996 / 12 = 83

Location 2:

Month	# of Part-Time Employees	# of FTEs (hours worked / 120) *Make sure to round down
January	10,000	10,000/120=83
February	10,000	10,000/120=83
March	10,000	10,000/120=83
April	10,000	10,000/120=83
May	10,000	10,000/120=83
June	10,000	10,000/120=83
July	10,000	10,000/120=83
August	10,000	10,000/120=83
September	10,000	10,000/120=83
October	10,000	10,000/120=83
November	10,000	10,000/120=83
December	10,000	10,000/120=83
Total:		996

Average yearly FTEs: 996 / 12 = 83

Location 3:

Month	# of Part-Time Employees	# of FTEs (hours worked / 120) *Make sure to round down
January	10,000	10,000/120=83
February	10,000	10,000/120=83
March	10,000	10,000/120=83
April	10,000	10,000/120=83
May	10,000	10,000/120=83
June	10,000	10,000/120=83
July	10,000	10,000/120=83
August	10,000	10,000/120=83
September	10,000	10,000/120=83
October	10,000	10,000/120=83
November	10,000	10,000/120=83
December	10,000	10,000/120=83
Total:		996

Average yearly FTEs: 996 / 12 = 83

Location 4:

Month	# of Part-Time Employees	# of FTEs (hours worked / 120) *Make sure to round down
January	10,000	10,000/120=83
February	10,000	10,000/120=83
March	10,000	10,000/120=83
April	10,000	10,000/120=83
May	10,000	10,000/120=83
June	10,000	10,000/120=83
July	10,000	10,000/120=83
August	10,000	10,000/120=83
September	10,000	10,000/120=83
October	10,000	10,000/120=83
November	10,000	10,000/120=83
December	10,000	10,000/120=83
Total:		996

Average yearly FTEs: 996 / 12 = 83

Location 5:

Month	# of Part-Time Employees	# of FTEs (hours worked / 120) *Make sure to round down
January	10,000	10,000/120=83
February	10,000	10,000/120=83
March	10,000	10,000/120=83
April	10,000	10,000/120=83
May	10,000	10,000/120=83
June	10,000	10,000/120=83
July	10,000	10,000/120=83
August	10,000	10,000/120=83
September	10,000	10,000/120=83
October	10,000	10,000/120=83
November	10,000	10,000/120=83
December	10,000	10,000/120=83
Total:		996

Average yearly FTEs: 996 / 12 = 83

Location 6:

Month	# of Part-Time Employees	# of FTEs (hours worked / 120) *Make sure to round down
January	10,000	10,000/120=83
February	10,000	10,000/120=83
March	10,000	10,000/120=83
April	10,000	10,000/120=83
May	10,000	10,000/120=83
June	10,000	10,000/120=83
July	10,000	10,000/120=83
August	10,000	10,000/120=83
September	10,000	10,000/120=83
October	10,000	10,000/120=83
November	10,000	10,000/120=83
December	10,000	10,000/120=83
Total:		996

Average yearly FTEs: 996 / 12 = 83

Location 7:

Month	# of Part-Time Employees	# of FTEs (hours worked / 120) *Make sure to round down
January	10,000	10,000/120=83
February	10,000	10,000/120=83
March	10,000	10,000/120=83
April	10,000	10,000/120=83
May	10,000	10,000/120=83
June	10,000	10,000/120=83
July	10,000	10,000/120=83
August	10,000	10,000/120=83
September	10,000	10,000/120=83
October	10,000	10,000/120=83
November	10,000	10,000/120=83
December	10,000	10,000/120=83
Total:		996

Average yearly FTEs: 996 / 12 = 83

Add up the yearly FTE average for each location:

$$84+83+83+83+83+83+83 = \boxed{582}$$

Total # of FTEs

This is the total number of FTEs that the non-profit organization employs.

Add the total number of FT employees and the total number of FTEs:

$$350 \text{ FT} + 582 \text{ FTE} = \boxed{932}$$

Large Employer!

Since this number is more than 50, the non-profit organization is considered a large employer under Obamacare and must offer healthcare coverage to all FT employees to avoid penalties. Now the non-profit organization needs to consider its options.

OPTION 1:

The non-profit organization can choose to not offer insurance and pay the penalty:

Penalty A = $2,000 x (# FT – 30)
Penalty A = $2,000 x (350 – 30)

Penalty A = $2,000 x (320)
Penalty A = $640,000 a year

If the non-profit organization decides to play, it needs to offer insurance that is affordable and of minimum value. The cost of offering individual health insurance to all FT employees that meets these requirements is hypothetically $6,000 a year for each employee:

$6,000 x 350 FT = $2,100,000 a year

If the non-profit has been offering insurance since March 23, 2010 and the plan has continuously covered at least one person, that plan is considered grandfathered. Since some Obamacare regulations don't apply to grandfathered plans, the non-profit organization should consult with its insurance agent to determine if the plan needs to be modified and how much that would cost.

OPTION 2:

If the non-profit organization cannot afford to offer affordable and minimum value insurance for $2.1 million a year, it can choose to offer a skinny plan. By offering a skinny plan that provides minimum coverage, the non-profit organization will avoid Penalty A because it is offering healthcare to its employees. However, if a FT employee goes to an exchange and receives a premium tax credit because employer health insurance doesn't provide minimum value (which a skinny plan doesn't) or isn't affordable, the organization will be penalized with Penalty B. Penalty B is based on the number of FT employees who receive a premium tax credit from an exchange, not the total number of FT employees. The organization would be betting that most employees will accept the skinny plan and not go to an exchange to get a premium tax credit. The fewer employees that get a premium tax credit, the less penalty B is.

Hypothetically, a skinny plan would cost the non-profit organization $1,200 per employee for a year:

$1,200 x 350 FT = $420,000 a year

$420,000 is the cost of offering skinny insurance if all FT employees enroll in it. Since the non-profit organization can still receive Penalty B, let's calculate the worst-case scenario. Remember, Penalty B can never be greater than Penalty A. So, the worst case scenario would be one in which the number of FT employees receiving premium tax credits from an exchange causes Penalty B to be the same as Penalty A. To determine how many employees receiving a premium tax credit would result in Penalty B being the same as Penalty A, take the total amount for Penalty A and divide it by $3,000: $640,000 / $3,000 = 213.33 FT. For simplicity, let's round the number down to 213 FT.

So, if 213 FT employees turn down the non-profit organization's skinny plan and receive a premium tax credit, Penalty B would be:

Penalty B: $3,000 x FT employees that receive premium tax credit
Penalty B: $3,000 x 213 FT employees that receive premium tax credit
Penalty B: $639,000 a year

Now, let's determine the cost of healthcare coverage for the other 137 FT employees:

$1,200 x 137 FT = $164,400 a year
Adding together Penalty B and the cost of skinny plan coverage

gives us the total amount the non-profit organization could pay when offering a skinny plan:

$639,000 + $164,400 = $803,400 a year

Remember, $803,400 is the most they will pay if they choose to offer skinny insurance to their full-time employees. If most employees accept the skinny plan, Penalty B will be much less, reducing the overall cost per year.

OPTION 3:

To reduce the cost of health insurance, or the cost of penalties, the non-profit organization can reduce its number of FT employees and increase its number of PT employees. However, this may increase turnover rates because many PT employees will probably continue looking for a job that offers healthcare coverage and more hours. For example, the organization reduces its number of FT employees to 300 and increases its number of PT employees to ensure it still has enough staff. Penalty A for not offering insurance would be:

Penalty A: $2,000 x (# FT - 30)
Penalty A: $2,000 x (300 - 30)
Penalty A: $2,000 x (270)
Penalty A: $540,000 a year

The cost of offering insurance would also decrease because the non-profit organization has less FT employees to offer coverage to:

$6,000 x 300 FT = $1,800,000 a year

So, the non-profit organization would pay $540,000 a year

in penalties for not offering insurance to 300 FT employees, or play and offer insurance that costs it $1.8 million a year. Remember, the non-profit organization also needs to consider the costs of an increased turnover rate. There will be additional costs for finding a new employee, and this should also play a factor in the decision to pay or play.

Now let's see how the numbers change when offering a skinny plan. Remember, these calculations are based on the non-profit increasing its number of PT employees and decreasing its number of FT employees. The skinny plan would cost:

$1,200 x 300 FT = $360,000 a year

While this would be the cost for offering 300 FT employees skinny insurance, there is still the possibility of a FT employee receiving a premium tax credit from an exchange, which would trigger Penalty B. Let's calculate the most expensive scenario. Since Penalty B cannot exceed Penalty A, the most expensive scenario would be one in which the number of employees who received a premium tax credit caused Penalty B to be the same as Penalty A. To figure out how many employees this is, divide the Penalty A amount by $3,000:

$540,000 / $3,000 = 180 FT

So, if 180 FT employees turn down skinny insurance and receive a premium tax credit from an exchange, the non-profit organization's Penalty B would be:

$3,000 x 180 FT = $540,000 a year

If 120 employees enrolled in the skinny plan, the cost of their coverage would be:

$1,200 x 120 = $144,000 a year

Adding together the cost of Penalty B and the cost of enrolling 120 employees in skinny insurance gives us the most expensive scenario of what the non-profit could pay under option 3:

$540,000 + $144,000 = $684,000 a year

Remember, all the examples under Option 3 lay out situations in which the number of FT employees was reduced, which resulted in lower costs for the non-profit organization.

OPTION 4:

 The non-profit organization could consider offering overtime to their current FT employees in order to reduce the number of FT employees it employs. While this will lower the cost of health insurance and penalties, it will increase the labor costs associated with FT employees. For example, using the information from Option 3, let's assume that the 300 FT employees now have to pick up the hours that the 50 FT employees used to work. Those 50 FT employees that are no longer with the company used to work 130 hours a month each. Combined, they worked 6,500 hours a month:

50 FT x 130 hrs a month = 6,500 hours a month

The FT employees are paid $13.00 an hour, so those 50 FT employees used to cost the company:

$13.00 x 130 FT = $1,690 a month for 1 FT employee

$1,690 x 50 FT = $84,500 a month for 50 FT employees

Now the other 300 FT employees will need to pick up those 6,500 hours a month. Since all of the non-profit organization's FT staff already works 40 hours per week, those 300 FT employees may be paid overtime:

$13.00 x 1.5 OT = $19.50 an hour

$19.50 x 6,500 hrs = $126,750 a month

The difference between paying overtime to the non-profit organization's FT employees and not reducing the number of FT employees is:

$126,750 – $84,500 = $42,250 a month

Over the course of a year, this adds up to:

$42,250 a month x 12 months = $507,000

It will cost $507,000 more to pay overtime to the FT employees. Next, we need to see if the reduced cost of healthcare coverage and penalties makes reducing the number of FT employees and increasing the amount of overtime worthwhile.

Offering health insurance that meets the requirements under Obamacare to 300 FT employees costs $1,800,000 a year. Adding this to the increased labor costs will help determine if reducing the number of FT employees by offering overtime is less or more expensive:

$1,800,000 + $507,000 = $2,307,000 a year

The cost for offering insurance to 350 FT employees (Option 1) is $2,100,000 a year. So in this case it is cheaper to offer all 350 FT employees health insurance instead of cutting the number of FT employees down to 300 and paying them overtime.

Let's see if the same applies to skinny plans. The skinny plan would cost the non-profit organization $360,000 for 300 FT employees. This plus the overtime pay will help determine if reducing the number of FT employees by offering overtime is less or more expensive when offering skinny insurance:

$360,000 + $507,000 = $867,000 a year

CONCLUSION

Offering skinny coverage to 350 FT employees (Option 2) will cost the non-profit organization $420,000 a year. Again, it is less expensive to offer all FT 350 employees skinny insurance instead of reducing the number of FT employees to 300 by offering overtime.

If the FT employees are salaried and exempt, no overtime may be required, but now salaried staff must work another 10 hours per week. This may increase turnover rates.

EXAMPLE 4

Sally is a large franchisee owner. She has 20 restaurant locations, each of which employs 10 FT employees and 40 PT employees that work an average of 110 hours a week. Since Sally owns all 20 locations, the locations are calculated together when determining large employer status.

Determine the number of FT employees for each month at each location.

Afterward, find the average number of FT employees for the year for each location by adding up the total of FT employees for each month and dividing by 12.

Location 1-20:

Month	# of Full-Time Employees
January	10
February	10
March	10
April	10
May	10
June	10
July	10
August	10
September	10
October	10
November	10
December	10
Total:	**120**

Average yearly FTs: 120 / 12 = 10

All 20 locations have a yearly average of 10 FT employees.

Add these yearly averages of FT employees for each location together:

10 + 10 + 10 + 10 + 10 +

10 + 10 + 10 + 10 + 10 = (200)

Total # of FTs

This is the total of FT employees that Sally employs.

Add up the total number of hours PT employees worked for each month at each location and then divide the total number of monthly hours worked at each location for each month by 120 to determine each month's FTE.

Once you calculate each month's FTE, add them up to get the yearly FTE average.

Locations 1-20:

Month	# of Part-Time Employee Hours Worked	# of FTEs (hours worked / 120) *Make sure to round down
January	4,400	4,400/120=36
February	4,400	4,400/120=36
March	4,400	4,400/120=36
April	4,400	4,400/120=36
May	4,400	4,400/120=36
June	4,400	4,400/120=36
July	4,400	4,400/120=36
August	4,400	4,400/120=36
September	4,400	4,400/120=36
October	4,400	4,400/120=36
November	4,400	4,400/120=36
December	4,400	4,400/120=36
Total:		720

Average yearly FTEs: 720 / 12 = 36

All 20 locations have a yearly FTE average of 36. Add up the yearly FTE averages at each location to get the total number of FTEs that Sally employs.

$$36 \; X \; 20 \; = \; 720$$

Total # of FTEs

Add the total number of FT employees and the total number of FTEs:

$$720 \; + \; 200 \; = \; 920$$

Sally is a large employer!

Since this number is more than 50, Sally is considered a large employer under Obamacare and must offer healthcare coverage to all FT employees to avoid penalties. Now, Sally needs to consider her options.

OPTION 1:

Sally can choose to pay Penalty A for not offering health insurance to her 200 FT employees:

Penalty A: $2,000 x (# FT – 30)
Penalty A: $2,000 x (200 – 30)
Penalty A: $2,000 x (170)
Penalty A: $340,000 a year

If Sally decides to play and offer insurance to her FT employees, it needs to be affordable and of minimum value. Hypothetically, such insurance would cost $6,000 for single coverage for a year per employee:

$6,000 x 200 FT = $1,200,000 a year

Sally must decide whether providing health insurance to all her FT employees is in her budget. If it isn't and she decides to pay the penalty, she might see an increased turnover rate because her employees might look for another job that does offer health benefits. If she has already been offering her employees health insurance that was in existence before March 23, 2010 and has continuously covered at least one person, then that insurance is grandfathered. Since some Obamacare regulations don't apply to grandfathered plans, Sally should consult with her insurance agent to determine if any benefits need to be added and what the resulting cost would be.

OPTION 2:

If providing insurance that meets all the Obamacare requirements is too expensive for Sally, she can choose to offer her FT employees skinny insurance plans. Skinny plans do not meet the minimum value requirements because they do not offer enough coverage. So, although Sally will not receive Penalty A, she might receive Penalty B if one or more FT employees receives a premium tax credit through an exchange. By offering a skinny plan, Sally is hoping most of her employees will not go to an exchange and receive a premium tax credit. Hypothetically, the cost of skinny insurance is $1,200 per employee per year. So, the cost if all 200 FT employees enroll in the skinny plan is:

$1,200 x 200 FT =$240,000 a year

The cost may increase if some of Sally's FT employees receive a premium tax credit from an exchange. Let's calculate the most expensive scenario. Since Penalty B cannot exceed Penalty A, the the most expensive scenario would involve enough FT employees receiving a premium tax credit so that Penalty B was the same as Penalty A. To determine how many FT employees that is, take the Penalty A amount and divide it by $3,000:

$340,000 / $3,000 = 113.3 FT. For simplicity, round down to 113 FT.

With this scenario, 113 FT employees turned down the skinny insurance and received a premium tax credit from an exchange. The other 87 FT employees enrolled in skinny coverage. The cost of Penalty B, which was triggered by the 113 FT employees receiving a premium tax credit, is:

Penalty B: $3,000 x FT employees that receive premium tax credit

Penalty B: $3,000 x 113 FT employees that receive premium tax credit

Penalty B: $339,000 a year

Now, let's determine the cost of offering skinny insurance to the other 87 FT employees:

$1,200 x 87 FT = $104,400 a year

The most Sally would pay in penalties and healthcare costs in this situation is:

$339,000 + $104,400 = $443,400 a year

This is the most expensive scenario when offering skinny plans. If most of Sally's employees chose to enroll in skinny insurance and not go to an exchange to receive a premium tax credit, then Sally's costs will be much lower.

OPTION 3:

Because Sally is only required to offer healthcare coverage to FT employees and penalties are based on the number of FT employees, she could lower her healthcare costs and potential penalties costs by cutting down her number of FT employees and increasing her number of PT employees. However, if she increases her number of PT employees, her turnover rates may rise because her employees will continue to look for FT jobs with health coverage.

For example, Sally lowers her number of FT employees to 150 and increases her number of PT employees to make sure she has enough staff to work the store . Penalty A for not offering insurance will be less than before because it is based on fewer FT employees:

Penalty A: $2,000 x (# FT – 30)
Penalty A: $2,000 x (150 – 30)
Penalty A: $2,000 x (120)
Penalty A: $240,000 a year

The cost of offering insurance would also decrease because Sally has to offer healthcare coverage to fewer FT employees:

$6,000 x 150 FT = $900,000 a year

This is compared to $340,000 for Penalty A for 200 FT

employees and $1,200,000 for offering healthcare coverage to 200 FT employees (Option 1).

Now let's take a look at the difference in the costs of offering skinny insurance to Sally's reduced number of FT employees:

$1,200 x 150 FT = $180,000 a year

Just as in Option 2, the possibility exists that Sally will receive Penalty B for not offering insurance of minimum value if an employee receives a premium tax credit from an exchange. Let's calculate the most she could pay in both health insurance costs and penalties. Since Penalty B cannot exceed Penalty A, the most Sally could pay would require enough employees receiving a premium tax credit to cause Penalty B to be the same as Penalty A. To figure out how many employees that is, divide the Penalty A amount by $3,000:

$240,000 / $3,000 = 80 FT

If 80 FT employees turn down skinny insurance and receive a premium tax credit from an exchange, the non-profit organization's Penalty B would be:

$3,000 x 80 FT = $240,000 a year

70 employees enrolled in the skinny plan, so the cost of their coverage would be:

$1,200 x 70 = $84,000 a year

Adding together the cost of Penalty B and the cost of enrolling 70 employees in skinny insurance gives us the most Sally might pay in penalties and skinny insurance costs:

$240,000 + $84,000 = $324,000 a year

Remember, all of the possibilities with Option 3 lay out situations in which the number of FT employees was reduced, which resulted in lower costs for Sally in terms of health insurance and penalties.

OPTION 4:

Another way to reduce the number of FT employees is to offer overtime. While it will reduce the number of FT employees that Sally has, it will increase her labor costs. Let's run some calculations using the information from Option 3, in which Sally has reduced her number of FT employees from 200 to 150. Those 50 FT employees who are no longer with the company used to work 130 hours a month each. Combined, they worked 6,500 hours a month:

50 FT x 130 hrs a month = 6,500 hours a month

The FT employees are paid $13.00 an hour, so those 50 FT employees used to cost the company:

$13.00 x 130 hrs = $1,690 a month for 1 FT employee
$1,690 hrs x 50 FT = $84,500 a month for 50 FT employees

Now the other 150 FT employees will need to pick up those 6,500 hours a month. Since all of Sally's FT staff already works 40 hours a week, those 150 FT employees will be paid overtime:

$13.00 x 1.5 OT = $19.50 an hour
$19.50 x 6,500 hrs = $126,750 a month

The difference between paying overtime to Sally's FT

employees and not reducing the number of FT employees is:

$126,750 – $84,500 = $42,250 a month

Over the course of a year, this adds up to:

$42,250 a month x 12 months = $507,000

So it will cost $507,000 more to pay overtime to the FT employees. Next, we need to see if the reduced cost of healthcare coverage and penalties makes reducing the number of FT employees and increasing the amount of overtime worthwhile.

In this example, offering health insurance that meets the requirements under Obamacare to 150 FT employees costs $900,000 a year. Adding this to the increased labor costs will help determine whether reducing the number of FT employees by offering overtime is less or more expensive:

$900,000 + $507,000 = $1,407,000 a year

The cost for offering insurance to 200 FT employees (Option 1) is $1,200,00 year. In this case it is cheaper to offer all 200 FT employees health insurance instead of cutting the number of FT employees down to 150 and paying them overtime.

Let's see if the same applies to skinny plans. The skinny plan would cost Sally $180,000 for 150 FT employees. This, in addition to the overtime pay, will help determine whether reducing the number of FT employees by offering overtime is less or more expensive when offering skinny insurance:

$180,000 + $507,000 = $687,000 a year

CONCLUSION

Offering coverage to 200 FT employees (Options 2) will cost Sally $240,000 a year. It is less expensive to offer all FT 200 employees skinny insurance instead of reducing the number of FT employees to 150 by offering overtime.

EXAMPLE 5

A large company has 50 locations, each of which employs 200 FT employees and 250 PT employees who work an average of 95 hours a month. Because one company owns all 50 locations, the locations are calculated together to determine large employer status.

First, the large company needs to determine the number of FT employees employed at each location for each month of the year.

Then, find the average number of FT employees for the year for each location by adding up the total of FT employees for each month and dividing by 12.

Locations 1–50:

Month	# of Full–Time Employees
January	200
February	200
March	200
April	200
May	200
June	200
July	200
August	200
September	200
October	200
November	200
December	200
Total:	**2400**

Average yearly FTs: 2400 / 12 = 200

All 50 locations have a yearly average of 200 FT employees.

Now add the yearly averages for each location together:

$$200 \times 50 = 10{,}000$$

Total # of FT employees

This is the total of FT employees for the large company.

Add up the total number of hours PT employees worked for each month at each location.

Then, divide the total number of monthly hours worked at each location for each month by 120 to determine each month's FTE.

Lastly, add up the FTEs for each month for each location and divide by 12 to get the yearly FTE average:

Locations 1–50:

Month	# of Part-Time Employee Hours Worked	# of FTEs (hours worked / 120) *Make sure to round down
January	23,750	23,750/120=197
February	23,750	23,750/120=197
March	23,750	23,750/120=197
April	23,750	23,750/120=197
May	23,750	23,750/120=197
June	23,750	23,750/120=197
July	23,750	23,750/120=197
August	23,750	23,750/120=197
September	23,750	23,750/120=197
October	23,750	23,750/120=197
November	23,750	23,750/120=197
December	23,750	23,750/120=197
Total:		2,364

Average yearly FTEs: 2,364 / 12 = 197

Add up the yearly FTE average for each location:

$$197 \times 50 = \boxed{9,850}$$

Total # of FTEs

This is the total number of FTEs for the large company.

Add the total number of FT employees and the total number of FTEs:

$$9,850 + 10,000 = \boxed{19,850}$$

Since this number is more than 50, the company is considered a large employer under Obamacare and must offer healthcare coverage to all FT employees to avoid penalties. Now the large company needs to consider its options.

OPTION 1:

The large company can decide to pay and not offer insurance to its FT employees. As a result, it would pay Penalty A:

Penalty A: $2,000 x (# FT – 30)
Penalty A: $2,000 x (10,000 – 30)
Penalty A: $2,000 x (9,970)
Penalty A: $19,940,000 a year

The large company could instead choose to play and offer insurance that meets the minimum requirements of Obamacare. Such insurance hypothetically costs $4,500 per employee for single coverage for a year. They will get a discount per employee as a large group.

$4,500 x 10,000 FT = $45,000,000 a year

The large company needs to decide what fits in its budget and is in the best interest of the company. If the company decides to just pay Penalty A and not offer insurance, its turnover rate will probably increase because employees will search for another job that does offer health benefits. This likelihood increases because individual shared responsibility begins in January of 2014, which requires every individual to have health insurance or be taxed. Employees will be looking to their employers for that insurance.

If the large company has been offering the same health insurance since March 23, 2010 and it has continuously covered at least one individual, it is considered grandfathered. Some of the Obamacare insurance regulations don't apply to grandfathered plans, so the large company will need to consult with its insurance agent to see if any benefits need to be added and what their potential costs are.

The large company could also consider self-insurance, in which the company sets aside money each month for a health fund and then covers its employees' healthcare needs with that money. Again, certain Obamacare regulations don't apply to self-insurance so the large company should consult an insurance agent to determine which benefits to offer and what the cost would be.

OPTION 2:

If providing insurance that meets Obamacare requirements is out of the large company's budget, it can offer its FT employees skinny insurance, which contains bare-bones coverage. While the large company will avoid Penalty A, it may receive Penalty B if at least one FT employee receives a premium tax credit from an exchange because employer insurance was not affordable or of minimum value. By offering its FT employees skinny insurance, the large company is hoping that most will accept the skinny plan so that the number of FT employees who go to an exchange is very low. The cost of skinny insurance might be around $1,200 per employee per year. The cost of offering skinny insurance to all its FT employees is:

$1,200 x 10,000 FT = $12,000,000 a year

Since the large company may still receive Penalty B if a FT employee receives a premium tax credit from an exchange, the cost for offering skinny insurance could increase. Since Penalty B cannot exceed Penalty A, so the large employer would pay the most in this scenario if the number of FT employees that received a premium tax credit caused Penalty B to be the same as Penalty A. To determine how many FT employees that is, take the Penalty A amount and divide it by $3,000:

$19,940,000 / $3,000 = 6,646.66 FT. For simplicity, round up to 6,647 FT.

Let's say that 6,647 FT employees went to an exchange and received premium tax credits. This would trigger Penalty B:

Penalty B: $3,000 x FT employees that receive premium tax credit

Penalty B: $3,000 x 6,647 FT employees that receive premium tax credit
Penalty B: $19,941,000 a year
Penalty B cannot be more than Penalty A, which is $19,940,000.

Round Penalty B down to $19,940,000 a year. Now, let's determine the cost of offering skinny insurance to the other 3,353 FT employees who enrolled in the employer coverage:

$1,200 x 3,353 FT = $4,023,600 a year

If the large company decided to offer its FT employees skinny insurance, the most it would pay in penalties and healthcare costs is:

$19,940,000 + $4,023,600 = $23,963,600 a year

This number could be smaller, especially if most employees accept the skinny plan and do not go to an exchange to receive a premium tax credit.

OPTION 3:

If the large company reduced its number of FT employees and increased its number of PT employees to compensate, its costs related to healthcare and potential penalties would decrease. This is because both the costs of healthcare and the penalties are directly related to how many FT employees the company employs. However, the company's turnover costs may increase because the PT employees will look for FT jobs.

To see the difference in healthcare and penalty costs with fewer FT employees, let's say the large company reduces its number of FT employees to 9,000 and increases its number of PT employees so that it has the same amount of labor coverage. Penalty A for not offering health insurance to FT employees will now be less:

Penalty A: $2,000 x (# FT - 30)
Penalty A: $2,000 x (9,000 - 30)
Penalty A: $2,000 x (8,970)
Penalty A: $17,940,000 a year

The cost of offering insurance to FT employees would also decrease because there are fewer FT employees:

$4,500 x 8,970 FT = $40,365,000 a year

The cost of offering skinny insurance to FT employees will also decrease due to the reduced number of FT employees:

$1,200 x 8,970 FT = $10,764,000 a year

Just as in Option 2, there is the possibility that the large company will receive Penalty B for not offering insurance of minimum value if an employee receives a premium tax credit from an exchange. Let's calculate the most the company could pay in both health insurance costs and penalties. Since Penalty B cannot exceed Penalty A, the most it could pay would require enough employees receiving a premium tax credit to cause Penalty B to be the same as Penalty A. To figure out how many employees that is, divide the Penalty A amount by $3,000:

$17,940,000 / $3,000 = 5,980 FT

In this situation, 5,980 FT employees turned down the skinny insurance while 3,020 FT employees enrolled in the skinny plan. If all of the 5,980 FT employees who turned down skinny insurance received a premium tax credit, Penalty B would be:

$3,000 x 5,980 FT = $17,940,000 a year

The 3,020 FT employees who enrolled in the skinny plan would cost the large company:

$1,200 x 3,020 FT = $3,624,000 a year

Adding together the cost of Penalty B and the cost of providing 3,020 employees skinny insurance gives us the most which the large company might pay in penalties and skinny insurance costs:

$17,940,000 + $3,624,000 = $21,564,000 a year

Remember, all of the examples under Option 3 lay out situations in which the number of FT employees was reduced, which resulted in lower costs for the large company in terms of health insurance and penalties.

OPTION 4:

The large company could also try to reduce its health insurance costs and potential penalties by decreasing the number of FT employees and offering overtime. The extra overtime costs will increase the large company's labor costs and will outweigh the benefits of reducing the number of FT employees. Using the information from Option 3, let's say the large company reduces its number of FT employees to 9,000. The 1,000 FT employees that used to be with the company had each worked 130 hours a month. As a result, the company now needs to offer 130,000 hours of overtime to the remaining FT employees to maintain the correct level of coverage:

1,000 FT x 130 hrs a month = 130,000 hours a month

The FT employees are paid $13.00 an hour, so the 1,000 FT employees used to cost the company:

$13.00 x 130 FT = $1,690 a month for 1 FT employee
$1,690 hrs x 1,000 FT = $1,690,000 a month for 1,000 FT employees

Now the other 9,000 FT employees will need to pick up those 130,000 hours a month. Since all of the FT employees already work 40 hours a week, they will need to be paid overtime for the extra hours:

$13.00 x 1.5 OT = $19.50 an hour
$19.50 x 130,000 hrs = $2,535,000 a month

The difference between paying overtime to the FT employees and not reducing the number of FT employees is:

$2,535,000 – $1,690,000 = $845,000 a month

Over the course of a year, this adds up to:
$845,000 a month x 12 months = $10,140,000

It will cost $10.14 million more to pay overtime to the FT employees. Next, we need to see if the reduced cost of healthcare coverage and penalties makes reducing the number of FT employees and increasing the amount of overtime worthwhile.

Offering health insurance that meets the requirements under Obamacare to 9,000 FT employees costs $40,365,000 a year. Adding this to the increased labor costs will help determine whether reducing the number of FT employees by offering overtime is less or more expensive than keeping those 1,000 FT employees:

$40,365,000 + $10,140,000 = $50,505,000 a year

The cost for offering insurance to 2000 FT employees (Option 1) is $45,000,000 year. In this case, it is cheaper to offer all 10,000 FT employees health insurance instead of cutting the number of FT employees down to 9,000 and paying them overtime.

Let's see if the same applies to skinny plans. The skinny plan would cost the large company $10,764,000 for 9,000 FT employees. This, plus the overtime pay, will help determine whether reducing the number of FT employees by offering overtime is less or more expensive when offering skinny insurance:

$10,764,000 + $10,140,000 = $20,904,000 a year

CONCLUSION

Offering coverage to 10,000 FT employees (Options 2) will cost $12,000,000 a year. Again, it is less expensive to offer all FT 10,000 employees skinny insurance instead of reducing the number of FT employees to 9,000 by offering overtime.

EXAMPLE 6

Joe owns two retail stores: a clothing store and a jewelry store. The clothing store employs 3 FT employees and 13 PT employees who work an average of 80 hours a month. The clothing store also hires 10 PT seasonal employees who work 100 hours a month for the months of June – August and November – January. The jewelry store employs 5 FT employees and hires 5 FT seasonal employees November – February. Since Joe owns both the clothing store and the jewelry store, the stores must be calculated together when determining large employer status.

Determine the number of FT employees for each month at each store. For now, exclude seasonal employees.

Afterwards find the average number of FT employees for the year for each store by adding up the total of FT employees for each month and dividing by 12.

Clothing Store:

Month	# of Full-Time Employees
January	3
February	3
March	3
April	3
May	3
June	3
July	3
August	3
September	3
October	3
November	3
December	3
Total:	36

Average yearly FTs: 36 / 12 = 3

Jewelry Store:

Month	# of Full-Time Employees
January	5
February	5
March	5
April	5
May	5
June	5
July	5
August	5
September	5
October	5
November	5
December	5
Total:	**60**

Average yearly FTs: 60 / 12 = 5

Add the yearly averages for each store together:

$5 + 3 = 8$

This is the total of FT employees that Joe employs.

Add up the total number of hours PT employees worked for each month at each store. For now, exclude seasonal employees. Then, divide the total number of monthly hours worked at each store by 120 to determine each month's FTE.

Clothing Store:

Month	# of Part-Time Hours worked	# of FTEs (hours worked / 120)
January	1,040	1,040 / 120 = 8
February	1,040	1,040 / 120 = 8
March	1,040	1,040 / 120 = 8
April	1,040	1,040 / 120 = 8
May	1,040	1,040 / 120 = 8
June	1,040	1,040 / 120 = 8
July	1,040	1,040 / 120 = 8
August	1,040	1,040 / 120 = 8
September	1,040	1,040 / 120 = 8
October	1,040	1,040 / 120 = 8
November	1,040	1,040 / 120 = 8
December	1,040	1,040 / 120 = 8
Total:		96

Average yearly FTEs: 96 / 12 = 8

Jewelry Store:

Month	# of Part-Time Employees	# of FTEs (hours worked / 120)
January	0	0 / 120 = 0
February	0	0 / 120 = 0
March	0	0 / 120 = 0
April	0	0 / 120 = 0
May	0	0 / 120 = 0
June	0	0 / 120 = 0
July	0	0 / 120 = 0
August	0	0 / 120 = 0
September	0	0 / 120 = 0
October	0	0 / 120 = 0
November	0	0 / 120 = 0
December	0	0 / 120 = 0
Total:		0

Average yearly FTEs: 0 / 12 = 0

The yearly FTE average for the clothing store is 8 and the yearly FTE average for the Jewelry store is 0.

Add up the yearly FTE average for each location:

0 + 8 = 8. This is the total number of FTEs that Joe employs.

Now Joe needs to determine whether he can exclude his seasonal employees from his calculations. He hires the same seasonal employees for the months of June, July, August, November, December, and January for his clothing store. He hires the same seasonal employees for the months of February, November, December, and January for his jewelry store.

Add up the total number of FT seasonal employees for each month at each store. Because Joe only hires PT seasonal staff at the Clothing store, he will have a "0" total FT seasonal employee count each month.

Clothing Store:

Month	# of Full-Time Seasonal Employees
January	0
February	0
March	0
April	0
May	0
June	0
July	0
August	0
September	0
October	0
November	0
December	0
Total:	0

Jewelry Store:

Month	# of Full-Time Seasonal Employees
January	5
February	5
March	x
April	x
May	x
June	x
July	x
August	x
September	x
October	x
November	5
December	5
Total:	20

Do not calculate the yearly average yet. First, Joe must determine whether he can exclude his seasonal employees from the large employer calculations. Add up the total number of hours PT seasonal employees worked for each month at each location and then divide the total number of monthly PT seasonal hours worked by 120 to determine each month's seasonal FTE. The clothing store employs 10 PT seasonal employees who work 100 hours in the months of June – August and November – January. This means there are 1,000 part-time seasonal hours worked during those months at the clothing store.

Clothing Store:

Month	Part-Time Seasonal Hours	# of FTEs
January	1,000	1,000 / 120 = 8
February	x	
March	x	
April	x	
May	x	
June	1,000	1,000 / 120 = 8
July	1,000	1,000 / 120 = 8
August	1,000	1,000 / 120 = 8
September	x	
October	x	
November	1,000	1,000 / 120 = 8
December	1,000	1,000 / 120 = 8
Total	6,000	48

Since the seasonal employees in Joes's clothing store work more than 120 days a year (4 months), they are not considered "seasonal" under Obamacare and must be included in his large employer calculations. He might be able to exclude the seasonal workers from the jewelry store, but only if their employment is the only reason his FT + FTE count reaches at least 50.

Because Joe only hires FT seasonal employees at the Jewelry store, he will have a total of "0" PT seasonal employees each month.

Jewelry Store:

Month	Part-Time Seasonal Hours
January	0
February	0
March	0
April	0
May	0
June	0
July	0
August	0
September	0
October	0
November	0
December	0
Total:	0

Remember, the clothing store's seasonal employees were not exempt, but the Jewelry store's seasonal employees were.

Now, let's look at a breakdown of the numbers of FTs, FTEs, and seasonal employees for each store:

Clothing Store:

Month	Total FT Employees	Total FTEs	Total Non-exempt Seasonal Employees	Total (Total FT + FTE + Total Seasonal)
January	3	8	8	19
February	3	8	x	11
March	3	8	x	11
April	3	8	x	11
May	3	8	x	11
June	3	8	8	19
July	3	8	8	19
August	3	8	8	19
September	3	8	x	11
October	3	8	x	11
November	3	8	8	19
December	3	8	8	19
Total	36	96	48	180

Jewelry Store:

Month	Total FT Employees	Total FTEs	Total Seasonal Employees	Total (Total FT + FTE + Total Seasonal)
January	5	x	5	10
February	5	x	5	10
March	5	x	x	5
April	5	x	x	5
May	5	x	x	5
June	5	x	x	5
July	5	x	x	5
August	5	x	x	5
September	5	x	x	5
October	5	x	x	5
November	5	x	5	10
December	5	x	5	10
Total	60	0	20	80

Clothing Store:

Total # of Employees
19
11
11
11
11
19
19
19
11
11
19
19

+

Jewelry Store:

Total # of Employees
10
10
5
5
5
5
5
5
5
5
10
10

=

Both Stores:

Total # of Employees
29
21
16
16
16
24
24
24
16
16
29
29

Since the seasonal employees at the jewelry store work less than 120 days (4 months) out of the year, and the number of seasonal employees does not cause the total FT and FTE count to go over 50 for any month, then the seasonal employees at the jewelry store can be excluded from the large employer calculations. Refer to Chapter 2 regarding the policy for seasonal employee exemptions.

Now, add the monthly total of employees for each store together. Then, divide by 12 to find the average for the year.

(29 + 21 + 16 + 16 + 16 + 24 + 24 + 24 + 16 + 16 + 29 + 29) / 12 = 21.7

Now, add the total FT and FTEs together:

8 FT + 8 FTE = 16

Add the total seasonal FTEs from the clothing store to the total number of FT and FTEs:

16 + 4 = 20

Since this number is less than 50, Joe is a not a large employer.

SMALL EMPLOYER TAX CREDIT OPTION:

Joe can choose to offer health insurance to his employees and potentially receive a small employer tax credit to help cover the insurance costs. First, he needs to determine the number of FTEs he has using the small employer tax credit method.

The 3 FT employees at the clothing store work 2,080 hours a year and the 5 FT employees at the jewelry store work 2,175 hours a year. The 13 PT employees at the clothing store work 1,000 hours a year. Joe can exclude his seasonal employees when calculating the small employer tax credit calculation, but only at the jewelry store, because they worked less than 120 days of the year. Joe has to include his seasonal employees from the clothing store, because they do work more than 120 days per year, therefore are not "seasonal" according to Obamacare.

First, add up the number of hours each employee worked for the year at each location, not exceeding 2,080 per employee:

Clothing store:

Employee	Hours Worked for the Year
FT Employee 1	2,080
FT Employee 2	2,080
FT Employee 3	2,080
PT Employee 1	1,000
PT Employee 2	1,000
PT Employee 3	1,000
PT Employee 4	1,000
PT Employee 5	1,000
PT Employee 6	1,000
PT Employee 7	1,000
PT Employee 8	1,000
PT Employee 9	1,000
PT Employee 10	1,000
PT Employee 11	1,000
PT Employee 12	1,000
PT Employee 13	1,000
Total:	19,240

Jewelry store:

Employee	Hours Worked for the Year
FT Employee 1	2,080
FT Employee 2	2,080
FT Employee 3	2,080
FT Employee 4	2,080
FT Employee 5	2,080
Total:	10,400

Total Hours Worked at Both Locations: 29,640

Divide the total number of yearly hours worked by 2,080 to determine the year's FTE:

29,640 / 2,080 = 14.25 FTE. Round down to 14 FTE.

Next, calculate the employees' average yearly wages (which must be below $50,000).

The 3 FT employees in the clothing store are paid $13 an hour. Their yearly wages are 2,080 hrs worked x $13 = $27,040. The 5 FT jewelery store employees are paid $15 an hour. Their yearly wages are 2,175 hrs worked x $16 = $34,800. The 13 PT clothing store employees are paid $8.50 an hour. Their yearly wages are 1,000 hrs worked x $8.50 = $8,500. Add up the employees' wages:

$27,040 + $27,040 + $27,040 + $34,800 + $34,800 + $34,800 + $34,800 + $34,800 + $8,500 + $8,500 + $8,500 + $8,500 + $8,500 + $8,500 + $8,500 + $8,500 + $8,500 + $8,500 + $8,500 + $8,500 + $8,500 = $365,620

Divide the sum by the number of FTEs:

$365,620 / 14 = $26,115.71. Rounding to the nearest thousand, the average yearly wages are $26,000.

Since the average of the yearly wages is below $50,000, Joe is eligible for a tax credit if he offers health insurance to his employees, and pays at least 50% of the deductible.

Now he needs to calculate how much his small employer tax credit would be and compare it with the cost of offering insurance to his employees.

Joe pays $48,000 in health insurance premiums for his employees each year ($6,000 a year for each of his 8 FT employees). The amount he would have paid if his costs were the same as the average premium costs in the state of Texas would be $41,776 ($5,222 a year for each employee). The average premium costs for each state can be found in the instructions for IRS Form 8941.

From this point on, Joe needs to use the lower of the two above numbers for his calculations. He will use the state average: $41,776.

Next, multiply the state average by the percent of the tax credit. Since we are calculating the tax credit for the year 2013, the percent is 35% or 0.35 for businesses:

$41,776 x 0.35 = $14,621.60

Next, Joe needs to determine how much the credit will be reduced since he employs more than 10 FTEs. Determine how many FTEs over 10 he has:

14 FTE - 10 = 4 FTE

Divide that by 15 and round to 3 decimal places:

4 / 15 = .266

Multiply that by the tax credit amount:

.266 x $14,621.60 = $3,899.09

Subtract the above total from the tax credit amount:

$14,621.60 - $3,899.09 = $10,722.51

Next, Joe needs to determine by how much he needs to reduce his credit since his employees receive more than $25,000 in average annual wages. Determine how much over $25,000 he pays:

$26,000 - $25,000 = $1,000

Divide that by $25,000 and round to 3 decimal places:

$1,000 / $25, 000 = .04

Multiply that by the tax credit amount:

.04 x $14,521,60 = $584.86

Subtract the result from the already reduced tax credit amount:

$10,722.51 - $584.86 = $10,137.65

Joe will receive a $10,137.65 tax credit to help pay for insurance. Therefore, the cost of offering insurance to his 8 FT employees for one year will be:

$48,000 - $10,137.65 = $37,862.35

CONCLUSION:

When determining whether he can afford to offer healthcare to his employees, Joe also needs to consider the costs of turnover. His turnover rate will probably increase if he doesn't offer health insurance because his employees with look for a job with health benefits.

EXAMPLE 7

A farm employs 3 FT employees throughout the year. For both the planting season (April – June) and the harvest season (October), the farm hires 40 FT seasonal workers and 35 PT seasonal workers who work an average of 65 hours a month.

First, the farm needs to determine the number of FT employees employed for each month of the year, excluding seasonal employees.

Find the average number of FT employees for the year by adding up the total of FT employees for each month and dividing by 12.

✅ **FT Calculation**

Month	# of Full-Time Employees
January	3
February	3
March	3
April	3
May	3
June	3
July	3
August	3
September	3
October	3
November	3
December	3
Total:	36

Average yearly FTs: 36 / 12 = 3

Now the farm needs to determine whether it can exclude its seasonal employees from the calculations. The farm hires the same seasonal employees for the months of April, May, June, and October.

Add up the total number of FT seasonal employees for each month:

Month	# of Full-Time Seasonal Employees
January	×
February	×
March	×
April	40
May	40
June	40
July	×
August	×
September	×
October	40
November	×
December	×
Total:	160

Next, add up the the total number of hours PT seasonal employees worked for each month and divide the total number of monthly PT seasonal hours by 120 for each month to determine each month's seasonal FTE.

Month	# of PT Seasonal Employees	# of FTEs (total hours / 120)
January	X	
February	X	
March	X	
April	2,275	2,275 / 120 = 18
May	2,275	2,275 / 120 = 18
June	2,275	2,275 / 120 = 18
July	X	
August	X	
September	X	
October	2,275	2,275 / 120 = 18
November	X	
December	X	
Total:		72

Now let's look at a breakdown of the number of FTs, FTEs, and seasonal employees:

Month	Total FT Employees	Total Seasonal FT Employees	Total Seasonal FTE Employees	Total (Total FT + Total Seasonal)
January	3	x	x	3
February	3	x	x	3
March	3	x	x	3
April	3	40	18	61
May	3	40	18	61
June	3	40	18	61
July	3	x	x	3
August	3	x	x	3
September	3	x	x	3
October	3	40	18	61
November	3	x	x	3
December	3	x	x	3

The seasonal employees work less than 120 days (4 months out of the year). During, the 4 months that they work, the FT + FTE mark only exceeds 50 because of the seasonal employees. Therefore, the farm does not need to include the seasonal employees in the large employer calculations.

Find the average number of FT employees for the year by adding together how many FT employees worked each month and dividing by 12.

(3 + 3 + 3 + 3 + 3 + 3 + 3 + 3 + 3 + 3 + 3 + 3) / 12 = 3 FT

This is the number of FT employees the farm employs. Since all PT employees are seasonal, the farm's FT+FTE is simply 3. Since this number is less than 50, the farm is a not a large employer.

SMALL EMPLOYER TAX CREDIT OPTION:

The farm can choose to offer health insurance to its employees and possibly receive a small employer tax credit. First, it needs to determine how many FTEs it employs using the small employer tax credit method, which uses the number of hours they worked for the year. This process is slightly different from the process of determining large employer status.

Employee	Hours worked for the year
FT Employee 1	2,080
FT Employee 2	2,080
FT Employee 3	2,080
Total:	6,240

The 3 FT employees work 2,080 hours a year. Since the seasonal employees work less than 120 days out of the year, they are not included in the small employer tax credit calculations.

Divide the total number of yearly hours worked by 2,080 to determine the year's FTE:

6,240 / 2,080 = 3 FTE

Next, calculate the employees' average yearly wages (which must be below $50,000):

The 3 FT employees are paid $14 an hour. Their yearly wages are 2,080 hrs worked x $14 = $29,120. Add up all the employees' wages, excluding seasonal employees, owners, etc:

$29,120 + $29,120 + $29,120 = $87,360

Divide the sum by the FTE:

$87,360 / 3 = $29,120.

Rounding to the nearest thousand, the average yearly wages are $29,000.

Since the average of the yearly wages is below $50,000, the farm is eligible for a tax credit if it offers health insurance to its FT employees.

The farm provided health insurance to its 3 FT employees and the insurance costs $6,000 per employee for one year of individual coverage. The total amount the farm paid for healthcare is:

3 FT x $6,000 = $18,000

Now, the farm needs to determine how much it would have paid for insurance if it was paying the average premiums for the state of Texas, where it is located. The average premiums can be found on the instructions for IRS Form 8941 and the average for Texas is $5,222. Multiply that by the 3 FT employees:

3 FT x $5,222 = $15,666

For the rest of the calculations, the smaller premium amount is what is used. So, in this case, the farm should use the state average premium amount because it is less than the actual amount the farm paid. Multiply the state average by the 35% tax credit (for the year 2013) or 0.35:

$15,666 x 0.35 = $5,483.10

Now the farm needs to determine how much its tax credit is reduced by since it pays its employees more than $25,000 average annual wages. To do so, the farm needs to determine how much more than $25,000 it is paying its employees:

$29,000 - $25,000 = $4,000

Divide the result by $25,000 and round to 3 decimals:

$4,000 / $25,000 = 0.16

Multiply 0.16 by the tax credit amount:

0.16 x $5,483.10 = $877.30

Subtract the result from the tax credit amount:

$5,483.10 - $877.30 = $4,605.8

This is the tax credit that the farm will receive. Let's subtract that from the overall health insurance costs for offering insurance to employees to determine what the farm will pay for health insurance:

$18,000 - $4,605.80 = $13,394.20

CONCLUSION

The farm was able to determine that offering insurance was within the budget.

EXAMPLE 8

A surf shop employs 2 FT employees year round. However, during the months of March, May – August, and December – January, the shop hires 5 FT seasonal employees and 10 PT seasonal employees who work 80 hours a month.

First, determine the number of FT employees employed for each month of the year, excluding seasonal employees:

✓ FT Calculation

Month	# of Full-Time Employees
January	2
February	2
March	2
April	2
May	2
June	2
July	2
August	2
September	2
October	2
November	2
December	2
Total:	24

Average # of FT employees: 24/12 = 2

The average number of FT employees for the year is 2.

Now the surf shop needs to determine whether it can exclude its seasonal employees from the calculations. The surf shop hires one set of seasonal employees for the months of March, April, and May, and another set of seasonal employees for the months of August, December, and January.

Add up the total number of FT seasonal employees for each month:

Month	# of Full-Time Seasonal Employees
January	5
February	5
March	5
April	5
May	5
June	5
July	5
August	5
September	5
October	5
November	5
December	5
Total:	60

Next, add up the the total number of hours the PT seasonal employees worked for each month and divide the total number of monthly PT seasonal hours by 120 for each month to determine each month's seasonal FTE.

Month	Hours worked by Part-Time Employees	# of Seasonal FTEs (Hours worked / 120)
January	800	800 / 120 = 6
February	x	
March	800	800 / 120 = 6
April	800	800 / 120 = 6
May	800	800 / 120 = 6
June	x	
July	x	
August	800	800 / 120 = 6
September	x	
October	x	
November	x	
December	800	800 / 120 = 6

Now let's look at a breakdown of the number of FTs, FTEs, and seasonal employees:

Month	Total FT Employees	Total Seasonal FT Employees	Total Seasonal FTE Employees	Total (Total FT + Total Seasonal)
January	2	5	6	13
February	2	×	×	2
March	2	5	6	13
April	2	5	6	13
May	2	5	6	13
June	2	×	×	2
July	2	×	×	2
August	2	5	6	13
September	2	×	×	2
October	2	×	×	2
November	2	×	×	2
December	2	5	6	13

Since the seasonal employees work less than 120 days (4 months) out of the year, and the FT and FTE count never goes over 50 for any month, so the seasonal employees can be excluded from large employer calculations. However, the surf shop wouldn't be a large employer even if the seasonal employees were included.

Add all the months' non-seasonal FT+FTE together and divide by 12.

Now, add the FT and FTEs together:

2 + 0 = 2

Since this number is less than 50, the surf shop is a not a large employer.

SMALL EMPLOYER TAX CREDIT OPTION:

Although the surf shop is not required to offer health insurance to its employees, it could potentially receive a small employer tax credit if it chooses to do so. First, it needs to determine whether it is eligible for the small employer tax credit.

Calculate the FTE using the small employer tax credit method. The 2 FT employees work 2,080 hours a year. Add their yearly hours together:

Employee	Hours worked for the year
FT Employee 1	2,080
FT Employee 2	2,080
Total:	4,160

Divide the total number of yearly hours worked by 2,080 to determine the year's FTE:

4,160 / 2,080 = 2 FTE

Next, calculate the employees' average yearly wages (which must be below $50,000):

The 2 FT employees are paid $12 an hour. Their yearly wages are 2,080 hrs worked x $12 = $24,960. Add up all the employees' wages, excluding the seasonal employees:

$24,960 + $24,960 = $49,920

Divide the sum by the FTEs:

$49,920 / 2 = $24,960

Since the average of the yearly wages is below $50,000, the surf shop is eligible for a tax credit if it offers health insurance to its employees.

The surf shop provides health insurance to its FT employees that costs $6,000 for single coverage for one employee a year:

2 FT x $6,000 = $12,000

Now the surf shop needs to compare that to the average cost of premiums (found on IRS Form 8941). The average premium for the state of Texas is $5,222, so the cost of providing insurance to 2 FT employees if the surf shop paid the average premiums is:

2 FT x $5,222 = $10,444

The lower amount is what matters, so from now on the surf shop needs to use the state average amount in its calculations. Take the state average and multiply it by the tax credit amount for 2013, which is 35% or 0.35:

$10,444 x 0.35 = $3,655.40

The surf shop does not have more than 10 FTE and does not pay its employees an average annual wage of more than $25,000, so it does not have to reduce its credit any further. Now let's determine what the cost of offering insurance to the FT employees is with the credit:

$10,444 - $3,655.40 = $6,788.60 a year

CONCLUSION

The surf shop needs to weigh the pros and cons of offering healthcare to its employees. When doing so, it needs to take into consideration that its turnover rate might increase if it doesn't offer insurance because its employees may look for a job with healthcare benefits.

13

It's estimated that Obamacare will cost trillions of dollars. Where is all that money going to come from? The government has imposed some new taxes and fees to help fund Obamacare.

ADDITIONAL MEDICARE TAX

The Additional Medicare Tax will help pay for the expansion of Medicare. It is a 0.9% tax on individuals who make more than $200,000 a year and married couples filing jointly that make more than $250,000 a year.[1] These taxes began January 1, 2013, and employers are responsible for taking the tax out of employees' paychecks.

BRANDED PRESCRIPTION PHARMACEUTICAL MANUFACTURERS AND IMPORTERS ANNUAL FEE

Companies that make more than $5 million creating and importing brand-name prescriptions are subject to this fee. The fee, which began in 2011, is divided among all companies

---

1   *Internal Revenue Service. (2013, May 8). Questions and answers for the Additional Medicare Tax. Retrieved from http://www.irs.gov/Businesses/Small-Businesses-&-Self-Employed/Questions-and-Answers-for-the-Additional-Medicare-Tax*

based on how much they sold compared to the rest of the market.[2] The projected total of the fees for 2011 was $2.5 billion; the projected total of the fees for 2012 and 2013 was $2.8 billion.[3]

CADILLAC TAX

Starting in 2018, a 40% excise tax will be applied to healthcare plans which annually cost more than $10,200 for an individual or $27,500 for a family. The insurer will be responsible for paying the tax for fully insured plans and the plan administrator will be responsible for paying the tax for self-funded plans.

EXCISE TAX ON INDOOR TANNING SERVICES

Since July 1, 2010, businesses that offer indoor tanning services were (and still are) required to collect a 10% excise tax from their customers.[4] The tax is then turned over to the government with the use of IRS Form 720.

HEALTH INSURERS ANNUAL FEE

Starting in 2014, health insurance providers will be required to pay a fee based on their net premium amount.[5] The fee is expected to generate $8 billion and will increase to $14.3 billion in 2018.[6]

---

2   *Department of the Treasury. (2011, August 18). Federal register. Re-trieved from http://www.gpo.gov/fdsys/pkg/FR-2011-08-18/pdf/2011-21011.pdf*
3   *Department of the Treasury. (2011, August 18). Federal register. Re-trieved from http://www.gpo.gov/fdsys/pkg/FR-2011-08-18/pdf/2011-21011.pdf*
4   *Internal Revenue Service. (2013, June 28). Indoor tanning services tax center. Retrieved from http://www.irs.gov/Businesses/Small-Businesses-&-Self-Employed/Indoor-Tanning-Services-Tax-Center*
5   *United Healthcare Services, INC. (2012, August 10). Insurer fee. Re-trieved from http://www.uhc.com/united_for_reform_resource_center/health_re-form_provisions/insurer_fee.htm*
6   *United Healthcare Services, INC. (2012, August 10). Insurer fee. Re-trieved from http://www.uhc.com/united_for_reform_resource_center/health_re-*

MEDICAL DEVICE EXCISE TAX

On January 1, 2013, a 2.3% tax on businesses that create or import medical devices was put into place.[7] Devices excluded from the tax are products which an individual can purchase in a store for individual use – such as glasses, contacts, and hearing aids.[8]

NET INVESTMENT TAX

Starting January 1, 2013, individuals who have a net investment income of more than $200,000 a year and married couples filing jointly with a net investment income of more than $250,000 a year will receive a 3.8% tax on investment income, estates, and trusts.[9]

PATIENT CENTERED OUTCOMES RESEARCH INSTITUTE (PCORI) FEE

This fee funds clinical research performed by the Patient Centered Outcomes Research Institute (PCORI). Employers that offer Health Reimbursement Accounts (HRAs) have to pay a fee of $1 per participant in 2013 and $2 per participant from 2014 through 2019. In addition, plan sponsors of self-insured plans and some insurance companies will be subject to the fee.[10]

---

form_provisions/insurer_fee.htm
7   *Internal Revenue Service. (2013, January 29). Medical Device Excise Tax. Retrieved from http://www.irs.gov/uac/Newsroom/Medical-Device-Excise-Tax*
8   *Internal Revenue Service. (2013, January 29). Medical Device Excise Tax. Retrieved from http://www.irs.gov/uac/Newsroom/Medical-Device-Excise-Tax*
9   *Internal Revenue Service. (2012, December 12). Net Investment Income Tax FAQs. Retrieved from http://www.irs.gov/uac/Newsroom/Net-Investment-Income-Tax-FAQs*
10   *Internal Revenue Service. (2013, June 7). Patient-Centered Outcomes Research Trust Fund fee (IRC 4375, 4376 and 4377): Questions and answers. Retrieved from http://www.irs.gov/uac/Patient-Centered-Outcomes-Research-Trust-Fund-Fee:-Questions-and-Answers*

TRADITIONAL REINSURANCE PROGRAM

The Traditional Reinsurance Program will be in place from 2014 to 2016. Its primary goal is to stabilize the individual market by helping cover high-cost individuals. All insurance companies and administrators of self-insured plans are required to contribute to the program.

CHAPTER REVIEW

- High-income individuals and couples will pay an additional Medicare tax on income.

- Companies that create and import brand-name prescriptions will pay an extra fee to the government.

- High-cost insurance will be subject to a Cadillac Tax of 40% starting 2018.

- Companies that offer indoor tanning services place an excise tax on those services.

- Companies that create and import medical devices will pay an extra fee to the government.

- Individuals and couples with high investment incomes will pay an additional 3.8% tax.

- Some employers, self-insured plans, and insurance companies will pay a PCORI fee.

- Insurance companies and self-insured plans will pay a Traditional Reinsurance fee.

14

QUESTIONS AND
ANSWERS

Q: If I split my business, will I no longer be a large employer?

A: No. Large employer status is determined on a group basis, which means that all the businesses that you are an owner of can potentially be calculated together. See Chapter 2 for more information.

Q: If I have 50 employees, am I automatically a large employer?

A: No. Large employer status takes into account full-time and part-time employees. The use of a full-time equivalent (FTE) calculation assesses the number of hours work by your PT employees by determining how many FT employees would be required to work the same number of hours. The full-time equivalent is combined with your number of full-time employees to determine whether you are a large employer. If you have more than 50 full-time employees and full-time equivalents, then yes, you are a large employer. See Chapter 2 for more information on large employer status.

Q: If I have less than 25 employees, do I automatically qualify for the small employer tax credit?

A: No. There are a couple of other factors to consider. Your employees can't make more than an average of $50,000 a year, and you have to pay for 50% of your employees' healthcare premiums in order to qualify for the small employer tax credit. See Chapter 8 for more information on the small employer tax credit.

Q: If I have 25 or more employees, am I automatically disqualified from the small employer tax credit?

A: No. Like large employer status, eligibility for the small employer tax credit takes part-time employees into consideration using a full-time equivalent calculation. To be eligible for the small employer tax credit, you must employ less than 25 FT + FTE employees. See Chapter 8 for more information on the small employer tax credit.

Q: Since the implementation of Obamacare's employer shared responsibility has been delayed, do my employees and I still have to have individual insurance to avoid penalty taxes?

A: Yes. Even though the employer shared responsibility component of Obamacare has been delayed, individual shared responsibility still takes effect January 1, 2014. Individuals without minimum essential healthcare coverage will receive a penalty tax. Exchanges are set to open in 2013, so insurance can be purchased there. See Chapter 8 for more information.

Q: What is minimum essential coverage?

A: Minimum essential coverage is coverage obtained from an acceptable employer-sponsored program, a health plan offered in the private market, a grandfathered plan, or a government-sponsored program that meets the minimal requirements of Obamacare (Medicare, Medicaid, some veteran plans, TRICARE, Children's Health Insurance Program, Health plans for Peace Corps volunteers, Non-appropriated Fund Health Benefits Program of the Department of Defense). See Chapter 3 for more information on minimum essential coverage.

Q: Since the implementation of Obamacare has been delayed, do I still have to provide insurance to my FT employees to avoid penalties in 2014 ?

A: No. Employer shared responsibility, which requires large employers to provide health insurance to their full-time employees, does not begin until January 1, 2015. However, if you intend to use the IRS lookback measurement method, you need to start your first measurement period in 2014. See Chapter 5 for more information on the IRS lookback measurement method.

Q: If I already provide insurance to employees, can I keep my current plan?

A: It depends. You can keep your plan if it is a grandfathered plan. While grandfathered plans may be exempt from some of the new insurance requirements, they are not exempt from all of them. Please consult your insurance agent to determine whether your plan complies with the new regulations. See Chapter 9 for more information on grandfathered plans.

Q: What will healthcare cost?

A: At the moment, it is difficult to foresee what the cost of healthcare will be. Insurance companies are in the process of submitting plans to exchanges for approval and we won't know what the exact costs are until the plans have been approved. However, many experts believe that premium costs will rise because insurance companies are required to offer more benefits for small group and individual insurance plans. See Chapter 9 for more information on insurance costs.

Q: Am I required to pay part of the insurance premiums for my employee's healthcare?

A: No. You are only required to offer insurance that is affordable, which means that the individual rate doesn't exceed 9.5% of an employee's W-2 wages. See Chapter 3 for more information.

Q: If I offer insurance to my full-time employees, am I penalty-free?

A: Not necessarily. If you are a large employer, and you offer insurance to all full-time employees, you will not receive Penalty A. However, if the insurance you offer is not affordable or not of minimum value, and at least one employee receives a premium tax credit, you will receive Penalty B ($3,000 x # of FT employees that received a premium tax credit). See

Chapter 3 for more information on penalties.

Q: Do I have to offer health insurance to my employees' spouses?

A: No. Large employers are only required to offer health insurance to employees' dependents. See Chapter 9 for more information.

Q: If an intern works more than an average of 30 hours a week or 130 hours a month, is the intern considered a FT employee?

A: Yes. The law makes no mention of interns, so you will need to provide insurance for them in order to avoid penalties. If you are a large employer and your interns work an average of more than 130 hours per month, they will be considered FT under Obamacare. However, keep in mind the contractor and seasonal exemptions in case any of your interns qualify as contractors or as seasonal employees. See Chapter 2 for more information on full-time employees.

Q: Do I have to know an employee's household income to make a plan affordable?

A: No. The IRS has created a safe harbor that allows you to use an employee's W-2 wages to determine if healthcare is affordable. See Chapter 3 for more information on guidelines regarding affordability. .

Q: If none of my employees are eligible for premium tax credits can I still receive penalties?

A: No. The penalties are based on employees that receive premium tax credits. If none of your employees are eligible for a premium tax credit, you won't receive a penalty. See Chapter 3 for more information on penalties.

Q: Can I avoid penalties by keeping my number of FT employees at 30 or below?

A: Maybe. You can avoid penalty A by keeping your number of full-time employees at 30 or below. This is because the penalty is calculated based on your number of full-time employees minus 30 (# FT - 30). However, you can still receive penalty B for not offering affordable and minimum value coverage. Penalty B is triggered when at least one employee receives a premium tax credit to help buy health insurance. See Chapter 3 for more information on penalties.

Q: How are penalties for not offering insurance determined?

A: Penalties will be based on the number of full-time employees who receive a premium tax credit through an exchange. The exchanges will contact you to inform you if one of your employees receives a premium tax credit. The IRS will then use information obtained from you and your employees to determine your penalty. See Chapter 3 for more information on penalties.

Q: If I offer healthcare to my FT employees and one of them doesn't accept it, will I receive a penalty?

A: As long as your healthcare coverage is affordable (costs the employee less than 9.5% of their W-2 wages) and of minimum value (the plan covers 60% of healthcare costs), then you will not receive a penalty. It is recommended that you have the employee sign a document that they opted out of your offered health coverage in case there are any disputes later. See Chapter 3 for more information on penalties.

Q: Do I have to do anything for 2014 since the implementation of Obamacare has been delayed?

A: You should start planning for the large employer calculation period now. The year 2014 will determine whether you are a large or small employer for 2015. Many companies are modifying their employment strategies and implementing those changes January 1, 2014.

If you plan to use the employer shared responsibility method to determine part-time and full-time status of employees, you will need to start the measurement period for your current employees in 2014 so that you can offer coverage to them in the stability period in 2015. If you plan to use a one year measurement period, you need to start preparing now. Employee notices, including the mandatory OMB form, will need to be issued starting October 1, 2014. See Chapter 5 for more information on using the IRS lookback measurement method.

Q: Can I have different lookback measurement periods for different employees?

A: Yes, but only for certain categories. You can have a different measurement, administrative, and stability period for employees in different bargaining agreements, employees in different states, employees with different union statuses (union v. nonunion), and employees with different salaried statuses (salaried v. hourly). See Chapter 5 for more information on the lookback measurement periods.

Q: Do I need to supply my employees with any notifications now that the implementation of Obamacare has been delayed?

A: Yes. All employers must provide a notification to their employees about the opening of exchanges. The Department of Labor has provided an example which contains information about what must be included in the notification. This notification form, OMB No. 1210-0149, can be found at: http://www.dol.gov/ebsa/healthreform/index.html and also on our website, www.EmployersandObamacare.com. See Chapter 6 for more information on employee notifications.

Q: If I am purchasing insurance for myself, do I have to purchase it through an exchange?

A: No. You can still purchase insurance through the private market, but keep in mind that insurance offered in the private market may not meet some of the requirements of

Obamacare, so you'll want to work with an agent. If you are going to purchase insurance through an exchange, keep in mind that you must purchase during the open enrollment period, which is October 1, 2013 – March 31, 2014. For 2014 and the years after, the open enrollment period will be from October 15 through December 7. See Chapter 8 for more information on your options as an individual.

Q: What's the deal with "30 hours per week" versus "130 hours per month" when determining FT status of an employee?

A: As with much of the rest of Obamacare, how to determine FT status hasn't been ironed out. According to IRS regulations, a FT employee is defined as an employee who works an average of 30 hours per week or 130 hours during a calendar month.

Throughout this book we use the monthly option to calculate FT status due to various clarification issues with the weekly option. It is difficult to calculate FT status on a weekly basis because there has not been a clarification of what a "week" is considered to be. Should the 30 hours per week be calculated based on the work week? The calendar week? If an employee is hired mid-week, should you "prorate" their hours that week? When calculating FT status using the IRS lookback measurement method, a period may not be an exact number of weeks long. The IRS has mentioned that the weekly average should be calculated on an annual basis. To do this you would add up all of the hours worked that year and divide by the number of weeks in the year, which is 52. To learn more about this, refer to Chapter 2.

TimeForge

TimeForge is a labor management software company, located in Lubbock, TX, that provides a suite of labor management tools for the restaurant, retail, and hospitality industries. Businesses around the globe use TimeForge's products as operational tools to plan and manage employee schedules, attendance, payroll, sales, reporting and human resources. TimeForge interacts with small and large businesses on a daily basis and is very familiar with their various day-to-day operations.

TimeForge was founded by Anthony Presley and Erik van Gilder in an effort to help businesses better manage and control their labor.

With TimeForge's vast experience with businesses of all sizes and labor management, they developed this handbook to help employers understand Obamacare, so businesses will be prepared for the employer mandate come 2015.

timeforge

ABC Advantage Benefits Connection

Advantage Benefits Connection is an independent insurance agency, located in Lubbock, Texas, which specializes in Health and Group Benefits for companies of every size. While our home office is in West Texas, we have experience dealing with multistate locations, and our team includes a licensed health advisor. ABC specializes in tailoring a benefits program that fits each client's individual needs, as well as budget. Whether you represent an individual or a company with 5 employees, 500, or 5000+ employees, ABC has the expertise you need. At Advantage Benefits Connection, we offer complete benefits administration for the individual, group core products, and group voluntary benefits. In addition, ABC can provide vital communication and enrollment completion for the benefit of employers and employees alike.

Advantage
Benefits
Connection

Anthony Presley

As the founder of TimeForge, Anthony works daily with the brains (the customers!) behind the best labor management software on the planet. Anthony's primary role is to ensure that the software that TimeForge produces does exactly what customers need, and that usually means dragging the HR department kicking and screaming into the world of iPhones, tablets, Facebook, and Twitter. It ain't easy.

Anthony and his partner, Erik, have worked together for over a decade, managing a variety of software projects for customers to keep their businesses humming along. The one unifying factor for these customers? Staffing problems, turnover, over-time, and labor issues plague each and every one. It didn't take long for the light bulb to click on, and TimeForge has been at the forefront of ensuring that employees of all generations get along just fine with the management (of all generations!).

Erik van Gilder

One of the founders of TimeForge.com, Erik has been at the forefront of helping managers and staff members remember that they want the same things. He works with upset managers and frustrated staff, and helps both groups see the light by upsetting and transforming the labor management processes in organizations. Smoothing communication between experienced managers and staff is what he does.

Previously, Erik ran a consulting company that helped transform human beings from mind-numbing dead-end jobs (fill out screen based on paperwork, click next, do again, click next, ... explode) into awesome customer-driven employees who have a customized computer program to help them do their job.

Erik's a native English speaker, which doesn't hurt. And, he loves History. Like, really, really loves History.

Jacqueline Kafka

Jacqueline was born and raised in New Mexico. She attended Texas Tech University and received a Bachelors in English and a minor in Spanish. While at TimeForge, she decided to pursue a law degree at the University of Arizona. She currently lives in Tucson, where she enjoys reading and dancing during her free time.

Audrey Presley

Audrey and her son live in Lubbock, where she's finishing her degree in technical writing with a minor in mass communications. She's worked with TimeForge since the company started, working first in technical support and blog writing, and now as a special projects manager. Audrey is an authority on labor management in the restaurant and retail industries, and helps customers maximize efficiency in their operations. Audrey is involved in various community organizations while keeping the hatches buttoned down at TimeForge.

Kevin Van

With 20 years of insurance and employee benefits experience, Kevin brings a wealth of knowledge regarding the health and insurance fields to the table. He has helped large, multi-state employers, medium size companies, as well as small businesses and their employees find affordable benefits that fit their individual and family needs. He has received numerous commendations for his exceptional work in his fields, being recognized both regionally and nationally.

Kristen Vander Plas

Kristen is an Honors graduate with a Bachelor's Degree in Humanities, a Specialization in Political Science, and minors in: English, History, and Law & Government. She earned the honor of Valedictorian and was selected as the first student commencement speaker in her Alma Mater's history. Currently, she is pursuing a Juris Doctorate at Texas Tech University School of Law, where she was named a Presidential Scholar for 2013. She is very experienced in the field of Social Media and employs it proficiently for organizations and various political campaigns.

Jessica Castner

Jessica Castner is a Senior Creative Fiction Writing and Philosophy student at Texas Tech University.

Born and raised in Lubbock, she has a special love for West Texas. She enjoys spending time with her three dogs, reading too much, and watching the same movies over and over. In addition to editing and writing portions of *Obamacare: A Handbook for Employers*, she writes and maintains content for the various media connections at TimeForge.

Rebecca Scott

Rebecca is a graduate from Texas Tech University, where she received a Bachelor's degree in Advertising. Rebecca stayed in Lubbock after graduating, enjoying the West Texas sunsets and the occasional haboob. She assists with the marketing of TimeForge products by keeping up with the social media and labor management trends in the restaurant, retail and hospitality industries. Rebecca manages to help customers find the right solutions for their businesses while improving marketing materials, illustrating manuals and books, and assisting with rebranding efforts.

www.ingramcontent.com/pod-product-compliance
Lightning Source LLC
Chambersburg PA
CBHW060351220326
41598CB00023B/2886

* 9 7 8 0 6 1 5 8 8 9 7 6 4 *